in producing policies to reduce the greenhouse gas emissions that
cause global climate change, has been revolutionary.'
Jay Inslee, Member of the United States
House of Representatives

'In the world of economic theory, Graciela Chichilnisky is an A-list star.'
Washington Post

'Graciela Chichilnisky has made important contributions to the
economic aspects of climate change, both in analysis and in the
formulation of appropriate policies. In particular, she has emphasized
the considerations of justice in a manner capable of reasoned analysis.
This book presents a lively account of the problem and the
perspectives of one who has played a significant and varied role.'
Kenneth Arrow, winner of the Nobel Memorial
Prize in Economic Sciences

'Graciela Chichilnisky is one of the most incisive minds working
on the subject of justice among the generations. In this book she and
Kristen A. Sheeran bring their remarkable analytical powers to the
practical problems that beset ongoing negotiations over climate
change . . . a wonderful piece of work.'
Sir Partha Dasgupta, Frank Ramsey Professor of
Economics at Cambridge University

SAVING KYOTO

An Insider's Guide to How it Works, Why it
Matters and What it Means For The Future

Graciela Chichilnisky and Kristen A. Sheeran
with a Foreword by Jean-Charles Hourcade

Contents

First published in 2009 by New Holland Publishers (UK) Ltd
London • Cape Town • Sydney • Auckland
www.newhollandpublishers.com

10 9 8 7 6 5 4 3 2 1

Garfield House, 86–88 Edgware Road, London W2 2EA, UK
80 McKenzie Street, Cape Town 8001, South Africa
Unit 1, 66 Gibbes Street, Chatswood, NSW 2067, Australia
218 Lake Road, Northcote, Auckland, New Zealand

ISBN: 978 1 84773 431 0

Senior Editor: Kate Parker
Editorial Direction: Rosemary Wilkinson
Commissioning Editor: Aruna Vasudevan
Cover design: Paul Wright
Design: Rebecca Longworth
Illustrations: Alan Marshall
Production: Melanie Dowland

Reproduction by Pica Digital Pte. Ltd., Singapore
Printed and bound by Replika Press in India

Foreword

'Timely', this is the word that immediately crossed my mind when I read Graciela's and Kristen's call to 'save Kyoto'. The international community is at this time facing a moment of truth because the additional greenhouse gases accumulated in the atmosphere since the Rio Conference in 1992 are such that the window of opportunity to stay below 'acceptable' levels of temperature increases is closing very quickly. But the Copenhagen UN climate change negotiations in late 2009 may lead to the same type of semi-failure as those at Kyoto if misunderstandings about how to frame the future climate regime are not cleared up. And one key source of misunderstanding may be the intellectual reflexes of the pro- and the anti-Kyoto.

I played a modest role in climate negotiations between Kyoto and the unfortunate COP6 in Den Hagen where the EU and the US, under Clinton's administration, failed to reach an agreement on how to enforce the Kyoto Protocol, the very month of George W. Bush's election. Although not so enthusiastic about the cap-and-trade approach explained in this book, I did my best to secure its success, at the minimum for a lack of anything better and hoping for more positive reasons. Graciela and other colleagues like Michael Grubb had indeed increasingly convinced me that something right could emerge from a system that I still find to be more complex than harmonized national carbon taxes.

I understand the skeptics of Kyoto, even though they have yet to formulate a comprehensive alternative that does not confront obvious political acceptability problems. The main danger, in my view, is not to question Kyoto and to search for an alternative to it, but, while doing so, to forget the intellectual roots of the Kyoto Protocol, its overall consistency and the deep political rationale for its emergence. This would lead us to lose time in desperate attempts to reinvent it or to be trapped in endless ideological disputes.

This book is thus timely because it helps us to avoid such traps by providing a clear understanding of what the Kyoto Protocol is, why it emerged and how it can be adapted to the current context. It provides real guidance for any reflection on the climate regime running up to (and continuing after) Copenhagen. Its great merit is to link very closely state-of-the-art analysis of the climate change problem, an explanation of the intrinsic economic, ethical and political logic of the cap-and-trade approach, a very well-informed long-term view of the negotiation process, an evaluation of the state of the carbon markets, and a clear diagnosis about the potential roadblocks to achieve a viable climate regime apt to deliver ambitious levels of avoided greenhouse gases emissions. The authors tackle major sources of deadlocks such as the false choice between trade and the environment, or the constraints imposed by the EU on carbon imports from the Clean Development Mechanism (CDM) – weakening a major incentive for developing countries to switch towards low-carbon development pathways, and undermining the political acceptability of any global deal.

As Graciela and Kristen write, Kyoto needs updating. Beyond technical (but important) issues such as the reformation of the CDM, this means adapting the Kyoto framework to a context characterized both by financial turmoil and a strong rebalancing of economic powers in the World. In some sense, the Copenhagen negotiations are untimely. The merit of cap and trade is to achieve wealth transfers between North and South, not through transfers of income but through uneven carbon constraints on countries. But even in the 1990s when the North/South division was almost synonymous with a Rich/Poor division, those transfers were not 'sold' to the public opinion in the North. Selling them now could prove even more difficult when the

North–Rich/South–Poor division is blurred by the fast emergence of China, India and to a lesser extent Brazil as candidate economic powers. But it may be, and this is the interest of Chapter 7, that the financial turmoil restores the timeliness of Copenhagen.

In this context, the reader should pay attention to the perspectives discussed in Chapter 7. It starts from the fact that the world economy needs mechanisms to build confidence and trigger massive investments to relaunch the world growth engine in a sustainable manner in a context of uncertainty. New global financial mechanisms linked to carbon markets could accelerate investments in carbon saving projects and, by the same token, contribute to this relaunching. This book suggests that the Kyoto approach may even be extended to other environmental problems in order to preserve ecological services while boosting economic development.

I do not have the answer to the question which ends the book: will the global community save Kyoto? I am sure, however, that those who sincerely want to promote development and upgrade world security in a world under climate constraint will benefit from a careful reading of a book that builds on the experience of one of the world's top economists. Graciela Chichilnisky perceived very quickly the importance of the climate affair, contributed to its intellectual framing and helped us, in a contact group between the US and the EU in the corridors of Kyoto, to write a text that was successful in clarifying the misunderstandings about the cap-and-trade approach on both sides of the Atlantic, thus paving the way for the Kyoto Protocol.

Jean-Charles Hourcade
Research Director, Centre National de la Recherche Scientifique (CNRS)
Director, Centre International de Recherche sur l'Environnement et le Développement (CIRED)
Convening Lead Author for the second and third reports of the Intergovernmental Panel on Climate Change (IPCC)

For our children

Introduction

We live in unusual times. Human settlements cover the entire planet and like hungry locusts we are drinking and eating our way through pastures, minerals, trees, rivers and oceans, as well as other species. In the process we are changing the planet's atmosphere, the oceans and the myriad of species that comprise life on earth. In doing so we are endangering our own life support systems. We are capable of creating great technologies but we are fouling our own nests. The crisis we have created is that we are destroying our own home.

Here is one way to see the problem: when we use energy to run a car or to heat our homes we generate carbon emissions that change the earth's atmosphere. Even exhaling causes carbon emissions. The impact was negligible when the earth housed a million people but now there are over six billion people sharing this planet and there may be three billion more by the year 2050. We know that the carbon emissions we produce are potentially dangerous. We run the risk of unleashing catastrophic climate change that will threaten the survival of all living systems, including our own. Never before has humanity confronted such an enormous challenge.

With every challenge comes opportunity. This book is about the challenge and the opportunity of climate change. The situation is difficult, but the future is actually very hopeful – if we find a way to get there.

You would think that with risks so serious we would be doing something about it. You would be right, and as it happens we *are* doing something. We reached one international agreement to forestall global disaster – the Kyoto Protocol of the United Nations. The Kyoto Protocol capped the emissions of the main emitters, the industrialized countries, one by one. It also created an innovative new financial mechanism, the carbon market and its Clean Development Mechanism (CDM), which has the potential both to reduce the emissions responsible for climate change and to transfer wealth and clean technology to poor countries.

The Kyoto Protocol is a historic agreement, the first of its kind. It creates a new market that is based on trade in user rights to the atmosphere – the global commons – which we all share. The Kyoto Protocol took 20 years of sweat and tears to build and is scheduled to expire in 2012. Like Cinderella's carriage, it turns into a pumpkin at the stroke of 12. The Kyoto Protocol is not perfect but it did succeed in getting almost all nations to cooperate to reduce global emissions. This is a good beginning. But unless we take action soon it will disappear into a puff of smoke. What do we do then? How do we save Kyoto?

First we need to understand how we dug ourselves into this hole, a topic we will look at in more detail in the first chapter. Essentially, the climate crisis comes from two centuries of industrialization, which expanded and accelerated after World War II and which depended heavily on fossil fuels – coal, oil and natural gas – to provide energy to the economy. Energy is the mother of all goods. Everything is made with energy. Economic development still depends on the availability of cheap energy sources and in today's global economy, this means fossil fuels. Fossil fuels generate roughly 87 per cent of the energy used in the world today.

The consequences of our thirst for fossil fuels are becoming increasingly apparent. The science is new and there are still uncertainties, but the risks are real. Glaciers are melting before our eyes. Entire towns in Alaska are sinking in the melting permafrost and warming seas.[1] According to the World Heath Organization (WHO), more than 150 thousand people die and five million more become ill each year because of climate change.[2] Ominous signs of a changing climate abound. Heat waves in western Europe that claimed 30 thousand lives in 2003, monsoons that left 60 per cent of Bangladesh underwater in 2004, and an increase in the frequency and intensity of Atlantic hurricanes, such as Hurricane Katrina, which wiped out much of the US's Louisiana and Mississippi Gulf Coast in 2005, are examples.

A Toxic Dependence

Yet our demand for fossil fuels continues unabated. China builds a new coal plant each week and the rest of the world builds two.[3] The average US consumer uses more energy today than ever before, despite advances in energy efficiency, and faced recently the highest oil prices since the Organization of the Petroleum Exporting Countries (OPEC) oil embargoes of the 1970s. The desire for energy independence has created powerful incentives for countries such as China and the US to use their abundant coal resources to meet their rapidly growing energy needs.[4] This is very bad news indeed, because coal is the worst of all the fossil fuels in terms of the amount of carbon it emits.

There is no simple solution to the climate crisis, no silver bullet that can rid us of our fossil fuel dependence. The Executive Director of the International Energy Agency (IEA), Nobuo Tanaka, believes we need an energy revolution. Tanaka says we need to change the world's energy infrastructure at a cost of $43 trillion, which is two-thirds of the gross domestic product (GDP) of the entire planet. It is safe to say that this change will not happen quickly. It is a race against time.

What is clear is that our grandchildren will inherit a world that is very different from our own. They will either inherit a planet with a severely diminished capacity to support human life or they will inherit a global economic system fuelled by cleaner, renewable energy sources that respects ecological limits and is capable of meeting the basic needs of every woman, man and child. Which path we set them on is entirely dependent on our response to this crisis. So much hangs in the balance.

We have the chance to transform this crisis into an opportunity for renovating the global energy infrastructure. The clean energy industry is growing rapidly. Investment in clean energy jumped 60

3

per cent between 2006 and 2007, as investors placed $150 billion in new capital into this emerging industry.5 This seems hopeful. Perhaps we can turn the crisis into a success story of human ingenuity and cooperation. But let us not get ahead of ourselves. The omens are not good and time is running out.

One critical problem for the future of the Kyoto Protocol is the impasse between the rich and the poor nations. The US, for example, has refused so far to ratify the Kyoto Protocol unless China, and possibly India, agrees to limit emissions. Unless the US, the world's largest greenhouse gas emitter, is included in the Kyoto Protocol, we will not be able to prevent climate change. How will the global community overcome this divide and forge cooperation between rich and poor countries, between the US and China?

In a nutshell, the question comes down to this: who should reduce emissions – the rich countries or the poor countries?

The rich nations depended heavily on fossil fuels to industrialize. Rich countries generate 60 per cent of the total emissions worldwide that are driving climate change, in order to feed and clothe less than 20 per cent of the world's population. Meanwhile, the rest of the world is left behind. Now poor countries say that it is their turn. Can we really ask poor countries to sacrifice their development opportunities now to atone for our sins of the past? Can we suddenly change the rules of admission to the club of industrialized nations by requiring countries to find a non-fossil fuel dependent path to development? We can try, but we may very well not succeed. Rich countries, and in particular the US, have little credibility at this stage, and many developing nations, such as India, China and Brazil, are beginning to flex their economic muscles.

There is a more basic issue at stake. The developing nations do not emit enough today to resolve the problem by themselves. Together the poor nations emit approximately 40 per cent of the world emissions (see 'Distribution of World Wealth, Population and Emissions' chart on p5). Africa, for example, emits only 3 per cent of the global emissions, South America approximately the same. Even if every woman, man and child in the developing nations, all five billion people, stopped emitting carbon today to oblige us they would still not make a dent in this problem. We need to reduce global emissions by at least 60 per cent, possibly 80 per cent, very quickly. Given who the big emitters are now, the only possible way to achieve this is to decrease emissions in the industrialized world. And this means us, the rich nations. There is no way to deny the problem. We must face our obligations squarely.

There is also the important issue of fairness to consider. The average person living in a rich country today produces far more carbon dioxide than her counterpart in a low or middle income

Distribution of World Wealth, Population and Emissions

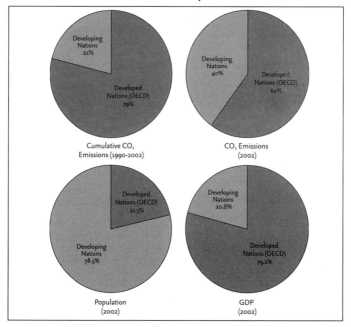

Source: World Resources Institute database earthtrends.wri.org, accessed 4 May 2007. World Bank Development Indicators 2007.

country. According to the World Bank, per capita emissions of carbon dioxide in 2004 averaged 0.9 metric tons in low-income countries, 4.0 metric tons in middle-income countries and 13.2 metric tons in high-income countries.[6] Should the countries that are most responsible for creating the global climate crisis take the lead in solving it? Should the countries that are best able to afford emission reductions shoulder more of the burden? The Kyoto Protocol answered yes to both of these questions and excused developing countries from mandatory emission cuts at this point in time. Can we sustain this commitment to fairness in the future?

At the same time, we need to be aware that 20 years from now developing nations could create catastrophic global warming for the entire planet by doing exactly the same that we did during our industrialization period: using their own resources to burn fossil fuels and emit carbon. This is why the solution to the climate crisis must involve us all.

This book explains why international cooperation between poor and rich nations is crucial in order to prevent catastrophic climate change. The stage for international cooperation has already been set. The Kyoto Protocol, the only international treaty to prevent climate change, has created a carbon market, which can unite the interests of poor and rich countries, environmental interests and business interests, to solve the climate crisis. Its unique properties will ensure that our efforts to prevent climate change are both fair and efficient. The carbon market – a market for a global public good – is distinct from any other market in history.

This book details the history of global climate negotiations that led to the Kyoto Protocol from the perspective of Graciela Chichilnisky, the architect of its carbon market. The Kyoto Protocol is scheduled to expire in 2012 and many difficult political and economic challenges lie ahead. The Kyoto Protocol is our generation's best hope for solving the climate crisis. Its success can provide a blueprint for implementing sustainable development and overcoming the global income divide. Will we save Kyoto?

Global Crisis

1

Global warming mesmerizes and polarizes public opinion. Climate change is on everyone's minds, yet most people do not fully understand it. Some even deny it. Confusion is understandable, after all, we have all observed changes in climate from one year to the next. We also know that the earth's climate has changed dramatically over the course of geological history. What is so different now to warrant such alarm?

The difference is that we may be now to blame for the changing climate. When scientists refer to climate change, they are talking about changes in the earth's climate, above and beyond natural climate variation, which has been caused, directly or indirectly, by human activity. The consequence of this activity alters the composition of the earth's atmosphere and causes average surface temperatures on earth to rise. The increase in the earth's surface temperature is known as global warming; global warming is driving climate change. Global warming can cause polar ice to melt and the seas to rise, by 64 to 80 metres (210 to 262ft) according to the US Geological Survey. If this happens a large part of the world we inhabit today will be under the sea, including Miami, New York City, Amsterdam, Tokyo and Shanghai (see 'Top 20 Cities Threatened by Coastal Flooding From Climate Change' table on p36).

When the sun's energy hits the earth a portion of that energy is reflected back into the atmosphere. Greenhouse gases in the atmosphere, gases such as carbon dioxide, methane, nitrous oxide, carbon monoxide and others, trap a portion of the heat released by the sun-warmed earth. This is called the greenhouse effect. Although human activity increases other greenhouse gases, carbon dioxide is the gas most responsible for global warming. Carbon emissions comprise more than 80 per cent of the greenhouse gases we produce and carbon emissions remain in the atmosphere for hundreds of years once emitted. For this reason, reducing carbon emissions is the primary focus of global warming prevention efforts. The solution may require us to reduce not just emissions but the actual stock of carbon that is stored in the atmosphere today, a technology known as negative carbon and described in Chapter 2.

The global carbon cycle is the way the earth balances the carbon exchange between air, oceans and terrestrial ecosystems (see 'The Global Carbon Cycle' diagram on p9). In pre-industrial times the earth maintained stable carbon dioxide concentrations in the atmosphere and warmed the earth to temperatures that modern human life is accustomed to. These are the temperatures that our bodies and agricultural systems evolved to live in and to thrive on. But the Industrial Revolution marked a turning point: it disrupted the global carbon cycle. We began pumping carbon dioxide into the atmosphere at a pace faster than the earth could regulate. We began a new era of rapidly increasing atmospheric carbon dioxide levels.

With the Industrial Revolution began our reliance on fossil fuels for industrial, transportation and home energy uses. This accelerated after World War II with the creation of the Bretton Wood Institutions, such as the World Bank, and the corresponding amplification of global trade. As we burn fossil fuels, such as coal, oil or natural gas, we release carbon dioxide emissions into the atmosphere. The largest emitters of carbon are the power plants that produce electricity for our homes and our factories. Power plants are responsible for 40 per cent of all emissions in the US and even more around the world. Transportation is a much smaller but significant contributor of emissions. Transportation accounts for approximately one-third of US emissions and 13 per cent of global emissions.

The Global Carbon Cycle

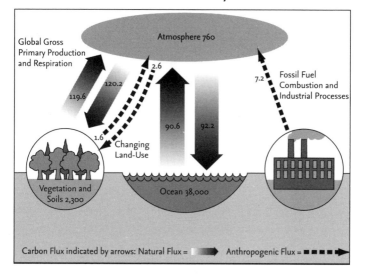

Global Gross Primary Production and Respiration

Atmosphere 760

2.6

120.2

119.6

1.6

Changing Land-Use

90.6   92.2

7.2   Fossil Fuel Combustion and Industrial Processes

Vegetation and Soils 2,300

Ocean 38,000

Carbon Flux indicated by arrows: Natural Flux =   Anthropogenic Flux = ■ ■ ■ ■ ➤

According to a recent United Nations Food and Agriculture Organization report, *Livestock's Long Shadow*, the various processes involved in bringing meat to the table (meat that is mostly consumed in the rich nations) together emit 18 per cent of all carbon emissions in the world,[1] more than the entire global transportation system. These emissions all intensify the greenhouse effect, increase global temperatures and may cause irreversible damage and rising seas.

Forest ecosystems play a critical role in the global carbon cycle. Through photosynthesis, forests sequester carbon dioxide from the atmosphere and store it. The carbon is released back into the atmosphere when trees die and decay. This is all part of the global carbon cycle. But when forests disappear faster than new forests grow, it disrupts the global carbon cycle and contributes to rising atmospheric carbon levels. The conversion of forests to alternative uses, such as when they are harvested for timber products or converted to arable land, releases much of the carbon that had been stored in the wood and the soil back into the atmosphere. This too has contributed to global warming, though to a lesser extent. Scientists attribute roughly 80 per cent of the increase in atmospheric carbon dioxide levels to burning fossil fuels and 20 per cent to land-use change and deforestation. Accounting for emissions from forestry is tricky because when trees die they release more carbon than they captured while alive.

The speed with which we are altering the earth's atmosphere is unprecedented. Since 1970, greenhouse gas emissions have increased by more than 70 per cent. The rate of increase in greenhouse gas emissions is now one hundred times higher than during the past 20 thousand years.[2] If emissions continue to grow at the same rate, atmospheric levels of carbon in the 21st century will double, and possibly triple, from pre-industrial levels.[3] As scientists are quick to warn us, we are heading rapidly into uncharted territory with very little geological history to guide us. We are driving a global experiment of unknown results. And we are near the point of no return.

So, what do we know for certain? The overwhelming scientific consensus is that average temperatures on earth are rising due to human causes. This is the assessment of the Intergovernmental Panel on Climate Change (IPCC), an international group of experts formed by the United Nations in 1988 to review the scientific research on climate change, its causes and its anticipated effects. Scientists know that average global temperatures rose by 0.74°C (1.33°F) last century. Eleven of the past twelve years were the hottest ever recorded. If atmospheric carbon dioxide levels double from their pre-industrial levels as is likely, temperatures could rise by as much as 4.5°C (8.1°F) over the next century. An even higher temperature increase has not been ruled out.[4]

At first thought, an increase in global temperature of 4.5°C (8.1°F) may not seem so serious. But small changes in average temperature can lead to significant climate effects. At the poles, temperatures change two or three times faster than they do in the rest of the world.[5] During the last Ice Age, glaciers covered most of

Canada and the northern US, but the earth was only 5°C (9°F) cooler on average then than it is now!

Tipping Points and Potential Catastrophes

What climatic changes do scientists now predict? The answer to this question is not straightforward. As much as we know about climate change, there is still much we do not know. The current and projected rates of warming are terrifying because they are without precedent over the last 20,000 years. Climate is a dynamic and complex system that is difficult to predict. It is not simply the case that the earth will keep getting a little hotter each year and that each year the effects will be just a little worse than they were the year before. If this were true we could anticipate impacts and prepare for them. Instead, scientists warn, there are likely to be critical thresholds or tipping points in the climate system. These are truly points of no return. Once we pass these thresholds, there is no turning back and the consequences could be dire. Complete collapse of the polar ice sheets or a change in ocean circulation – both of which are possible – would cause abrupt and catastrophic changes that no living or economic system could quickly adapt to. If all of the ice sitting on land in Greenland and Antarctica melted, global sea levels would rise by 64 to 80 metres (210 to 262ft).[6] That is enough for most cities in the world to disappear under the sea, certainly Miami, New York and Amsterdam among others (see 'Top 20 Cities Threatened by Coastal Flooding From Climate Change' table on p36). The Organisation for Economic Co-operation and Development (OECD) recently ranked the largest cities at risk from sea level rise from climate change and Miami and Shanghai were close to the top of the list with losses of $3.5 trillion and $1.7 trillion respectively. The OECD damage estimates for cities alone includes $35 trillion in property losses.[7] This is 50 per cent of current world economic output and yet only accounts for property damage – not loss of human life.

Scientists do not know exactly where the tipping points in the global weather system are because natural systems are highly sensitive to change and they are interrelated in so many complex ways. The earth's climate has never warmed this rapidly, by our own doing. We have no previous experience to draw on. We are playing a game of Russian roulette with our climate system and the longer we play, the more likely it is that our luck will run out.

Researchers still know relatively little about feedback effects that might either increase or weaken the pace and effects of climate change. For example, the permafrost regions in Russia and Alaska contain high concentrations of methane, a greenhouse gas that, if released into the atmosphere, could accelerate the greenhouse gas effect. Western Siberia, which is one of the fastest warming places on earth, holds the world's largest peat bog, a region of permafrost the size of France and Germany combined, which was formed at the end of the last Ice Age. It is melting, and scientists fear it could release as much as 70,000 tonnes of methane over the next several decades. Similar melting has occurred in eastern Siberia as well.[8]

The earth is large, and there is enormous momentum of hot air and water behind global warming. It cannot be stopped and turned around on a dime. Because carbon pollution is so long-lived in the atmosphere, the emissions we are pumping out now will continue to affect the earth for hundreds of years. The damage caused by human interference in the climate system may not be fully apparent for many years in the future. Warming by at least 2°C (3.6°F) by the end of the century is almost inevitable. We are already experiencing damage today, such as species extinction and the sinking of Alaska under the warming seas. Scientists have identified 12 diseases deadly to humans and wildlife that are spreading their geographical range due to climate change. These include avian influenza, Babesiosis, Cholera, Ebola, intestinal and external parasites, Lyme Disease, plague, Red Tides, Rift Valley Fever, Sleeping Sickness, Tuberculosis and Yellow Fever.[9] Australia, the oldest of all the continents, began an epic drought in 2002 that has claimed hundreds of lives from wildfires with no end in sight as of early 2009.

If the global community acts fast to reduce carbon emissions we may be able to prevent additional damage. But to do this, we will have to reduce global emissions by roughly 60–80 per cent of their current levels by 2050. This is no easy task, but it is certainly worth doing. It is still possible. We may no longer be able to prevent climate change, but we can still prevent *catastrophic* climate change. Climate scientist Martin Parry warns, 'We now have a choice between a future with a damaged world or a severely damaged world.'[10] It is really just a question of degree.

Climate Change Impacts

Predictions of future climate change impacts range from significant and disruptive, to potentially catastrophic. Many are surprised to learn that some of the most serious effects of the carbon pollution we spew into the air will be felt in the sea. Increased carbon uptake by the world's oceans has made them more acidic. This is expected to damage fragile marine ecosystems, especially corals and the many species that depend on them. About 50 per cent of the coral in the Caribbean is already gone.

Warmer temperatures cause the seas to expand. Warmer temperatures also speed the melting of the polar ice caps. These two forces combined have already led sea levels to rise by 10–20cm (4–8in) from pre-industrial times. And because it takes so long for the oceans to cool, sea levels will continue to rise for centuries. Global sea levels rose by 1.8mm (0.07in) each year between 1961 and 2003. Since 2003, increased melting of the Greenland and Antarctic ice sheets pushed the rate of sea level rise to 3.1mm (0.12in) each year. Complete melting of the Greenland and Antarctic ice sheets could increase sea levels to the extent that many coastal cities and island nations will be submerged and millions of people will be displaced. Bangladesh and the Maldives will disappear and New York will sink beneath the waves. The Greenland ice sheet is now disappearing at more than twice the rate that scientists initially feared. Total collapse of the Greenland ice sheet is unlikely this century, but not impossible.[11]

When glaciers melt, they infuse the oceans with fresh water. This can damage fragile marine ecosystems and may disrupt ocean currents such as the Gulf Stream, which plays a crucial role in distributing heat on earth. Rising sea levels can contaminate underground fresh water supplies, contributing to an already existent shortage of drinking water worldwide. Rising sea levels have already contaminated underground water sources in many small island nations, as well as in Israel, Thailand, the Yangtze Delta in China and the Mekong Delta in Vietnam.

The impacts of climate change have also been felt on land. In Alaska and Russia, where air temperatures have risen twice as fast as global mean average temperatures, the permafrost layer of soil is melting, causing significant structural damage and sinking entire towns into the warming seas. In the mid to high latitudes of the northern hemisphere, snow cover has already decreased by 10 per cent. The 20th century witnessed a two-week decline in the annual duration of lake and river ice-cover. Glaciers, which contain most of the planet's freshwater supplies, are retreating the world over. Switzerland, for example, recently lost two-thirds of its glacier volume. Polar bears that depend upon the ice to find food may soon become extinct.

A warming world may also witness major changes in precipitation, torrential rains, draughts, hurricanes and typhoons. Arid and semi-arid regions can anticipate more severe droughts and desertification while other parts of the world can expect increased rainfall and flooding. This could prove disastrous for regions of the world already suffering from acute food shortages. The most dramatic declines in agricultural productivity are predicted for Africa and Latin America, where food is most needed. Early studies of climate impacts suggested substantial agricultural gains in higher latitudes, as a result of longer growing seasons and the fertilizing effects of higher carbon levels on crops. The results of more recent field studies, however, predict that overall crop yields will decline, even in regions where yields were once predicted to rise, such as the US, China and Canada.[12]

Climate change is expected to increase both the frequency and severity of extreme weather events such as hurricanes, cyclones, heat waves and monsoons. Just as no single case of lung cancer can be blamed on smoking, no single storm can be blamed on climate change. However, many scientists interpret severe weather patterns in recent years as signs of climate change unfolding. The Rhine floods of 1996 and 1997, the Chinese floods of 1998, the East European floods of 1998 and 2004, the Mozambique and European floods of 2000, heat waves in western Europe in 2003, monsoon flooding in Bangladesh in 2004 and hurricane Katrina in the Atlantic in 2005 may be sobering reminders of more powerful weather events to come as our planet continues to warm.

Even the most conservative predictions of climate impacts suggest that most living systems will be adversely affected. Climate change poses indirect threats to human life, by decreasing food and fresh water supplies and expanding the range of some vector-borne diseases, such as malaria and dengue fever. Catastrophic weather events, droughts and heat-related illnesses pose more direct threats. It is hard to believe that 35 thousand people perished in Europe during the heat wave of August 2003 – one of the hottest summers ever recorded in Europe. It is a sobering example of how vulnerable even the citizens of advanced modern economies are to unexpected climate changes. Fifteen thousand people died in France alone, where summer temperatures are generally mild and hospitals, retirement homes and apartment buildings lack air conditioning.[13] Public heath officials had no emergency protocols in place to deal with the crisis. Climate change has left public health and emergency officials worldwide scrambling to find the resources and the expertise to deal with climate-related disasters they never thought they would have to cope with. Sadly, this adaptive capacity is most lacking in the developing world, where the effects of climate change will be the severest.

Climate change will disrupt ecosystems and their ability to provide critical ecosystem services, such as air, water and food, which are essential for human health and well-being, and it will contribute to wide-scale extinction of plants and animals. Up to 30 per cent of plant and animal species are at risk of extinction if the average temperatures worldwide exceed 1.5–2.5°C (35–37°F).[14] We can already observe these effects. As northern climates become more like those of the south, some plant and animal species are shifting their ranges. Butterflies, dragonflies, moths, beetles and other insects are now found in higher latitudes and altitudes where it was previously too cold for them to survive. Such changes can disrupt ecosystems in very damaging ways. Across the western US and Canada, climate change has led to unprecedented outbreaks in mountain pine beetles, resulting in widespread forest loss. The forest loss, in turn, reduces carbon uptake and increases emissions from the decay of dead trees.[15]

Rapid climate change has even led to genetic and behavioural changes in some animal species. For example, in Canada the red squirrel now reproduces earlier in the year and increasing numbers of Blackcaps from central Europe spend the winter in Britain rather than the Mediterranean. But not all animal and plant species will be able to adapt. Species with longer lifecycles and smaller populations, such as polar bears, will experience a decline in their population as their food supply disappears with the changing climate.[16] It is difficult to predict how well living systems will adapt to changing climate patterns in the future. If warming is rapid and extensive enough, and circumstances and human settlements block their migration, plants and animals may not be able to adapt. Among the animals that may be most affected will be humans.

Can We Adapt to Climate Change?

Unlike other living things that have always had to adapt to their environment in order to survive, we have altered our environment throughout our history. Can we now adapt to the climate changes we have unleashed? No one really knows the answer to this question. What we do know is that the more extensive the warming and the more rapid its onset, the less time there will be to adapt and the more dangerous the impacts will be.

We also know that adaptation must occur in a world that is already severely stressed. Population growth, deforestation, soil erosion, desertification and wide scale extinction have diminished our resistance, leaving us more vulnerable to the effects of climate change. Our loss of natural storm barriers such as barrier islands, sand dunes and mangrove forests, nature's first line of defence against tropical storms, increases the magnitude of property damage from storms. We saw this first hand with Hurricane Katrina in New Orleans, where almost all of the natural storm barriers had been destroyed.

Hundreds of millions of people live in areas that will be inundated when sea levels rise, such as the Nile Delta in Egypt, the Ganges–Brahmaputra Delta in Bangladesh, the Maldives, the Marshall Islands and Tuvalu. Increased population density along the coasts is not just something we observe in the developing world. In the US, the migration to coastal cities and towns continues. More than half of the world's population now lives within 60km (37 miles) of the sea.[17]

Billions of people worldwide already lack access to clean drinking water. Even industrialized countries expect fresh water shortages in the coming decades as water demand continues to outstrip available supplies. By 2025, one-third of all people on the planet will face severe and chronic water shortages.

Climate change will intensify droughts, famine and disease in areas of the world where millions of people – most of them children – are already engaged in a desperate struggle for survival. Asia and Africa have suffered from an increase in frequency and intensity of droughts in recent years. By 2020 it is predicted that 75–250 million Africans will be exposed to increased water stress – when the demand for water exceeds the available amount – due to climate change. Six million children, the majority of whom live in developing countries, die from malnutrition each year. In Bangladesh, one of the countries that will be hardest hit by climate change, 900 children already die each day from starvation. Wheat production in India is already in decline because of climate change. In some African countries, the increase in droughts is expected to reduce agricultural production by as much as 50 per cent.[18]

Climate change will increase the spread of diseases such as malaria and dengue fever, which already claim millions of lives each year in developing countries. According to the World Health Organization, climate-sensitive diseases are among the largest global killers. Diarrhoea, malaria and protein-energy malnutrition alone cause more than 3.3 million deaths globally each year and 29 per cent of these deaths occur in Africa.

Climate change will prove most devastating to the world's poor and will kill more people in poor countries in Africa, South Asia and Latin America than elsewhere. Extreme weather events are already more common in these areas. Population density in Asia, Africa and Latin America is very high, so when disaster strikes, more people feel it. Poor countries typically lack the resources – medical, rescue and evacuation systems – to cope effectively with natural disasters. Death tolls are extraordinarily high as a result. In 2007, natural catastrophes claimed 15,000 lives worldwide, 11,000 in Asia alone.[19] Cyclone Sidr caused more than 3,300 deaths in Bangladesh. Weather-related natural disasters killed 600 thousand people worldwide in the 1990s. Of those deaths, 95 per cent were in poor countries.

Herein lies the first cruel irony of the climate crisis. The countries least responsible for producing greenhouse gases – the developing countries – are the countries now at greatest risk of death and human suffering because of climate change. The UN predicts that hundreds of millions of people in developing nations will face natural disasters, water shortages and hunger due to the effects of climate change.[20] Africa, which produces only 3 per cent of global emissions, is the most vulnerable continent to climate change because of multiple stresses and its lack of the capacity to adapt to change.[21]

The rich industrialized countries emit 60 per cent of global greenhouse gases, even though they make up less than 20 per cent of the world's population. Their industrialization led to the build up of carbon in the atmosphere. But if poor countries now follow their carbon-dependent path to economic development, the effects of climate change will almost certainly be disastrous.

This is the second great irony of the climate crisis: for the first time in history, the welfare of rich nations will depend directly on decisions made in poor nations in Africa, Asia and Latin America. These nations have the capacity to inflict trillions of dollars in losses in rich countries just by industrializing and using their own fossil fuels as rich countries did and continue to do. The challenge facing the global community is how to quickly reduce carbon emissions without leaving poor countries behind. The solution will demand nothing short of full cooperation between rich and poor countries. We have never achieved this in the past. Can we do it now? The Kyoto Protocol provides a chance to unite rich and poor countries against climate change.

Summary – What We Know

For too many years we have lulled ourselves into a false sense of security by treating the climate crisis as if it were still 'uncertain'. It is true that the science is still relatively new and we can not be sure about all aspects of climate change. We do not know for sure by how much the earth will warm, or how fast or how soon we will experience the impacts, or how bad those impacts will be and how well living systems can adapt. But we do now know more about climate change and we have greater consensus today than we do about most other scientific or social problems, such as quantum mechanics or monetary policy. In fact there is an alarming degree of consensus worldwide about the causes and effects of the climate crisis. Very few things about climate change are uncertain at this point. And what is still uncertain may not become clearer to us until it is already too late.

Most importantly there is no longer any doubt that we can cause climate change. We cannot deny the devastating impacts our economic activities could have on our planet and the crisis we have brought on ourselves to solve. All we can do is work cooperatively with other nations to find the solutions. And we must do it quickly. Scientists keep finding more evidence that warming is occurring faster, and that the effects are manifesting sooner than previously anticipated. As one imminent climate scientist warns, 'we are all

used to talking about these impacts coming in the lifetimes of our children and grandchildren. Now we know that it's us.'[22]
Here is a summary of what we know about climate change:

- Most scientists believe that average temperatures on earth are rising because of humans.
- Burning fossil fuels is responsible for the observed increase in warming over the last century, according to most scientists.
- The emissions we are pumping into the atmosphere now will affect the earth for hundreds of years.
- To avoid catastrophic risks, global carbon emissions must decline by roughly 80 per cent by the year 2050. According to the IEA, this requires an energy revolution involving $43 trillion in investments in new power plants.
- The consequences of climate change range from disruptive to potentially catastrophic, with economic damages as great as 20 per cent of global GDP at stake.[23] The OECD reports that climate change will cause $35 trillion in damages to the largest cities in the world.
- The ability of living systems to adapt to climate change will depend on the speed and severity of warming.
- Industrialized countries are most responsible for the risks.
- Poor countries are at the greatest risk of loss of life, property damage and human suffering from climate change.
- In the future poor nations could inflict trillions of dollars in damages on industrial nations simply by using their own fossil fuels to grow their economies the way we do today.
- There are some things we may never know about climate change until it is too late. Time is not on our side. We will soon reach the point of no return.
- If the ice sheets of Greenland and Antarctica melt, this will increase the sea level by 64–80 metres (210–262ft), according to the US Geological Survey, flooding most coastal areas in the world and displacing millions of people.

Insuring The Future

2

Climate change is a real risk. It has the potential to inflict catastrophic losses on the world economy and its people. A crisis this serious demands immediate action, so why is it so difficult to convince countries to do more to prevent climate change when the science is so compelling?

The reason is that the problem involves the use of energy – the key to all economic production in the world and the mother of all markets. Furthermore there is no simple solution to the problem. As Albert Einstein said, 'problems can't be solved by the same mindset that created them.' To solve the climate crisis we need to fundamentally rethink what it is that we produce and how we produce it. This basic truth is unsettling to many. It is hard to imagine a world that is not powered by fossil fuels. Wind farms, negative carbon, hydrogen cars, solar panels – the technologies of the post-carbon economy sound as if they come straight out of a science fiction novel. But this is not science fiction. The survival of the next generations is at stake. Our children understand that it is their world that we are changing. The future is now.

The Energy Dilemma

Energy is implicated in every life process. It is the single most important input in human production, especially in industrial societies. Until recently we haven't had to consider the implications of our energy use. To solve climate change, however, we need to transform our energy use and our energy sources. We need to think about energy in new and innovative ways. We need to consider the impacts of our energy use on living systems today and in the future.

In pre-industrial societies human energy was the main energy source. Our physical capacity to do work was our only real energy constraint. The Industrial Revolution then gave rise to machines powered by wood, coal and petroleum. Our use of these energy sources was constrained only by our ability to find and access them. For a long time the supply of fossil fuels seemed virtually unlimited. The world's population was small, only 700 million at the start of the industrial era, and new technologies were rapidly advancing that would improve our ability to discover and extract fossil fuels. The consequences of burning fossil fuels and destroying the world's forests were mostly unknown to us. The scale of human production was small compared with the earth's capacity to absorb and recycle the waste we generated as by-products. We never considered the possibility of ecological limits to growth. We believed that nature was ours to conquer.

The Industrial Revolution enabled a dramatic rise in living standards and as living standards improved, population and consumption increased. By 1800 the world population was one billion, by 1927 it had doubled. At the turn of the 20th century the world population hit six billion. As the number of the people on the planet grew exponentially, so too did the demand for energy, resources and land. The scale of human production grew large compared with the earth's carrying capacity.

By the second half of the 20th century it became apparent that we were approaching certain ecological limits. Not only were we using up resources at a pace that was not sustainable, but we were generating too much waste. Whispers of an emerging environmental crisis could be heard. The signs were palpable: we were choking on smog in London and Los Angeles and many rivers in the US were so heavily polluted with chemicals that they were actually catching on fire, such as the Charles River in Boston and the Cuyahoga River in Ohio. A new consciousness of the ecological impacts of human production was emerging, and out of that the modern environmental movement was born.

Climate change, however, was still a distant concern for most people. Scientific understanding of climate change, its causes and its impacts was still tenuous. The extraordinary toll that our fossil fuel dependence was taking on all living systems was not well understood. We were far more concerned with energy independence and diminishing energy supplies than we were with climate change. Some scientists had predicted that fossil fuel production, especially oil production, would 'peak' by the 1970s, at which point demand for oil would increase faster than the supply of oil worldwide. The economic impacts of dwindling fossil fuel supplies loomed large in our minds.

Today, however, we understand that there is a problem far more serious and immediate than diminishing oil supplies. We must transform our energy needs and energy sources. By the time the last drop of oil is extracted from the ground – whether that is in 25 years or 125 years – climate change may have made us abandon fossil fuels as our major energy source in order to save lives and property. But getting there will be an enormous challenge.

Fossil fuels generate roughly 87 per cent of the energy used in the world today.[1] They are the main source of carbon emissions. The most valuable of these fossil fuels is petroleum. Petroleum fuels our transportation systems and it is the basis for the plastic materials that are universally used today. Electricity itself is mostly generated by fossil fuels. Power plants that produce electricity from fossil fuels are the single largest source of emissions on the planet, representing 41 per cent of all emissions in the US.

Economic development depends on the availability of energy sources and right now, this still means fossil fuels (see graph on p51). Across history and across all nations of the world, there is a clear and direct connection between energy use and economic output. A country's industrial production can be measured by its use of energy. Today, any attempt to restrict carbon emissions involves reducing energy use. Until low cost alternatives to fossil fuels are developed, reducing emissions may mean reducing economic output.

Transforming the global economy will create winners and losers. It may destroy businesses that make large profits generating carbon emissions, while creating new profit opportunities where none previously existed. Improvements in energy efficiency will save households and businesses money and improve productivity. Smart investors already sense these opportunities. According to a recent United Nations' report, the amount of new investment capital flowing into renewable energy worldwide each year grew from $8 billion in 2005 to $100 billion in 2006, to a record $150 billion in 2007, with little signs of this trend abating. This 'gold rush' is on track to produce investment levels as high as $450 billion per year by 2012 and $600 billion by 2020.[2] As long as gains to some sectors offset losses to others, there will be no net loss to the global economy from our efforts to prevent climate change. The global economy may even be more robust, if the looming threat of financial disaster from the damages of climate change is removed.

The Solution Must Be Global

In February 2006, the British Prime Minister at the time, Tony Blair, summed up the issue succinctly by saying that the problem with global warming is that 'no nation in the world would voluntarily agree to reduce its economic growth'.

Blair is right: trying to reduce global carbon emissions is not an easy political or economic task. To significantly reduce emissions we will need to rethink how we power our factories, fuel our vehicles and heat our homes. It may even require changes in our lifestyles – where we live, what we buy, and how we spend our leisure time. With appropriate planning and investment in energy efficiency and alternative energy sources, we can reduce our dependence on fossil fuels without compromising our quality of life. But this means tackling the climate crisis head-on, rather than scrambling after-the-fact. But which country will go first?

The truth is no country will voluntarily reduce its emissions, unless other nations agree to follow suit. This one fact, as crude as it may sound, is the single most important reason why we need all nations to sign up to a global agreement on climate change. Of course, there are compelling ethical reasons why nations should cooperate to solve climate change. As citizens of the earth, we all share the responsibility to preserve the earth's climate system upon which we all depend. However, this ethic alone will not convince countries to reduce emissions as much as they need to in order to prevent climate change; at least it certainly hasn't thus far.

Why is it that the climate crisis demands a global response? There are many other environmental issues that capture international attention but do not necessarily require an international agreement to solve them. The destruction of the Amazon rainforest is a good case in point. All nations have a strong interest in preserving the Amazon rainforest because of its unparalleled diversity of plant and animal species and its ability to produce oxygen. Only the countries that contain the Amazon rainforest within their borders, however, have any real power to prevent its destruction. If Brazil adopts measures that encourage deforestation or turns a blind-eye to illegal logging, there is little the international community can do. It cannot intervene in the resource management decisions of a sovereign nation, despite the implications of those decisions for the global community. Other countries can encourage forest conservation in Amazonia by applying political pressure, providing financial support or by discouraging the consumption of Amazon forest products by their own citizens, but ultimately there is little that most countries can do directly to stop deforestation in the Amazon.

Climate change is different. In this case, all nations are implicated since all nations produce carbon emissions. And carbon emissions transcend borders. Global warming is the result of cumulative global emissions. The atmosphere does not distinguish between emissions from the US or China and the atmospheric concentration of carbon is the same all over the world. Carbon emissions have the same impact on global climate no matter where they are produced. It also doesn't matter where we reduce carbon emissions. A tonne of carbon reduced in the UK is as valuable for preventing climate change as a tonne of carbon reduced in India.

Avoiding climate change is a perfect example of a global public good.3 A global public good is something that once it is provided benefits all countries and no country can be excluded. Emissions reduction by any one country helps all countries to the extent that it may lower the risk of climate change. Countries pay the cost associated with their own emissions reduction but share the benefit with the rest of the world. But what incentives do countries have to provide global public goods? Countries do not always behave altruistically.

No country alone produces enough emissions to cause global warming. No country alone can stop it. Even if the US, the world's largest greenhouse gas polluter, eliminated all of its emissions, global emissions would only decrease by 25 per cent. This would be a huge step in the right direction, but emissions reductions by other countries would still be needed.

This is why a global agreement to reduce carbon emissions is so critical. No country has an incentive to reduce emissions, since doing so will not prevent climate change unless other countries do the same. To make it worthwhile for a country to cut its emissions, its actions need to be part of a larger, coordinated global effort that has the potential to stop global warming. An international climate treaty gives countries the assurance that their emissions reduction efforts will not be in vain. Emissions reductions will be costly. An international climate treaty gives countries more bang for their buck.

So why has it been so difficult to forge an international agreement to prevent climate change, when it is in every country's best interests to do so? Why hasn't the US ratified the Kyoto Protocol?

Free Riding

We know that without a global agreement to reduce emissions, climate change will continue unchecked. The damages from climate change will be significant – potentially catastrophic – for all countries, even though some countries may be harmed more than others. We also know that no single country can prevent climate change. This is why no single country will voluntarily curb its emissions. Without a doubt, all countries benefit if an international agreement reduces the threat of climate change. All countries should prefer this outcome to its alternative: no treaty and dangerous climate change. But there is a third outcome that countries may prefer even more that we have not yet considered. It is called free riding.

Free riding is the option that lets a country think that it can have its cake and eat it too. Here's how it works: if all countries bar one cooperate to avert climate change, the one country that does not cooperate benefits from the efforts of the rest of the world, without having to reduce its own emissions. It reaps all of the benefit without any of the sacrifice. Some might call this behavior despicable, but it is rational response to the incentives as they exist. It makes sense for any one country to attempt to free ride, either by opting out of a climate treaty or negotiating within a treaty to do as little emissions reduction as possible. But if one country thinks it makes sense to free ride, all countries think it makes sense to free ride. And if all countries attempt to free ride, we can't solve the climate crisis.

An international climate treaty such as the Kyoto Protocol helps overcome the tendency toward free riding by identifying each country's role in solving the climate crisis. But even it can't solve the problem entirely, since it can't force countries to honour their commitments. We don't have international governance that is capable of this type of enforcement. When the US walked away from the Kyoto Protocol process in 2001, after years of negotiation, there was little the international community could do in response. To its credit the global community remains committed to solving the climate crisis, with or without US participation.

Before we get too discouraged, let us remember that the global community has proven itself capable of negotiating solutions to major global environmental problems. The Kyoto Protocol is not the first international environmental agreement. Perhaps the best example of successful global cooperation to solve a trans-boundary pollution problem is the Montreal Protocol on Substances that Deplete the Ozone Layer. The Montreal Protocol phased out the use of ozone-depleting chemicals, thereby protecting the ozone layer from further deterioration. However, there were many factors working in favour of international cooperation in the case of the Montreal Protocol that are not present in the case of climate change. For one, there was more agreement and a better understanding of the causes of ozone depletion. Also, the consequences, especially the rise in skin cancers, posed an immediate and direct tangible threat to the inhabitants of rich industrialized countries. Secondly, from the perspective of industrialized countries, the benefits of protecting the ozone layer far exceeded the costs of eliminating ozone-depleting substances, even if they had to act alone without the help of other countries. Finally, the role of developing countries in the process was much less debated, since rich countries were the major producers of ozone depleting substances.[4]

In contrast, negotiating the Kyoto Protocol involved more controversy and setbacks. And negotiations going forward will be anything but smooth. The Kyoto Protocol is a global landmark, perhaps the most important international agreement of our times. Together with the Montreal Protocol, these two global protocols created important precedents for resolving global environmental problems. The Kyoto Protocol gives us our best chance for solving the global climate crisis.

How to Price the Future: An Economic Perspective

There are many issues that lend themselves to a straightforward comparison of the costs and benefits of taking action. Unfortunately, climate change is not one of them. A cost–benefit comparison assumes that costs and benefits can be measured in monetary terms with a reasonable degree of confidence. The costs of emissions reduction, in principle, involve well-defined monetary expenditures that we can count. The benefits of preventing climate change, however, are generally more difficult to measure and to quantify. The benefits of preventing climate change are the avoided damages from climate change: lives and property saved. The problem is that many of these benefits are intrinsically priceless and unpredictable.

Economists have long struggled with the problem of how to assign meaningful monetary values to seemingly priceless things such as human life, health and ecosystems. Is a human life worth $6 million or $600 million? Ask any one person and they are likely to tell you that their life is priceless. Is a life saved in the US more valuable than a life saved in India, because of the differences in expected lifetime earnings? Are polar bears worth more than Boyd's forest dragon, an Australian lizard expected to lose 20 per cent of its habitat from climate change, simply because more people recognize polar bears and think they are cute? The answers to these questions may seem somewhat arbitrary – and they are. The problem of assigning meaningful monetary values to things that are not usually bought and sold in the marketplace plagues all cost–benefit analysis. The problem, however, is particularly acute in the case of climate change, given the enormous potential for lives lost, plant and animal extinction and disruption to natural ecosystems.[5]

Discounting The Future

Even if we could all agree on a number that captures the benefit of saving lives, ecosystems and property from climate change, there is another fundamental problem to consider. Most of us will not witness the worst ramifications from climate change in our lifetimes. But our children might, and our grandchildren most certainly will, feel the impacts. The actions we take, or don't take, will have a much greater impact on those who are not yet born than on us. It is not just our own welfare at stake. Are we willing to pay today what it costs to ensure the welfare of future generations?

Almost everyone can identify a tendency to 'discount' the future in decision-making. We prioritize our present needs and desires and place less weight or significance on what may happen later on. The same logic applies in economics. It is common to treat a dollar of income earned today as more valuable than a dollar of income in the future. A bird in hand is worth two in the bush, is it not? We can invest our dollar today at a positive rate of interest and have more than a dollar in the future. We may be richer in the future, in which case a dollar will be worth less to us then than it is now. We may simply be impatient – we would rather consume with our dollar now rather than wait until later. These are all reasons why we may discount the benefit of saving future generations from climate change and place more emphasis on what it will cost us today to stop it.

It is a standard practice in financial markets to discount the short-term future. A dollar paid next year is worth less than a dollar in hand today: this is why we pay interest on a bank loan. But the practice of discounting can paralyze us from taking action on global warming, which has long-term effects. Through discounting we greatly underestimate the costs we inflict and literally obliterate our concern for future generations. For example, if we cause $1 billion in global warming damages in the year 2011, these damages are worth $940 million in 2010 at a standard 6 per cent discount rate and the same damages inflicted just one year later, in 2012, are only worth about $888 million in 2010. The value of these damages drop with time and decrease exponentially: $1 trillion in damages 100 years from today is a mere $3 billion today at a 6 per cent discount rate. This is less than oil companies' earnings in one year and does not appear to merit much global attention. The problem is about the same no matter what discount rate we use: 6 per cent, 5 per cent, or even 2 or 1 per cent. Using any discount rate, discounting decreases exponentially the dollar value today of the costs we inflict on future generations.

Is it appropriate to discount the welfare of future generations? Economists have long struggled with this question. The best known article on this subject was written in 1928 by Frank Ramsey, in which he argued, 'It is assumed that we do not discount later enjoyments in comparison with earlier ones, a practice which is ethically indefensible and arises merely from the weakness of the imagination.'[6]

It may be appropriate to discount the future if we believe that future generations will be much wealthier than we are now and better able to cope with the effects of climate change. But what if they are not wealthier? If we don't take action soon to prevent climate change, we will bequeath to our children and grandchildren a planet severely diminished in its capacity to support human life and economic activity. In which case, the dollar we think is more valuable to us now could actually be worth much more to them. We should give them more, not less, since conditions may be so much worse because of climate change. For the first time in the history of industrialized nations, the next generation may not surpass the living standards of the current generation. Progress may be reversed. Human extinction may be at stake.

But even if we were to assume that future generations will be as rich as we are, there is still little justification for highly discounting the future damages of climate change. Most of us would not consider our granddaughter to be less precious than our daughter, simply because she was born a generation later.[7] If we want to sustain our planet's ability to support future generations, we need to invest in climate change prevention now. Discounting may make sense for certain financial decisions but we can't let the tendency to discount skew our perception of the urgency of reducing emissions in the present, not when the future health of the planet and the welfare of our children, and their children, is at stake.

Evaluating Risk

How can we evaluate the risks to future generations? Climate change presents risks that are poorly understood, dependent on our actions, collective and irreversible. How can we determine what cost is worth incurring when the risks we face from climate change are unknowable in advance?

Managing climate risk is not a new activity. Indeed, environmental uncertainty, such as weather risk, is the oldest form of uncertainty. In medieval England, a peasant farmer's land was broken into many widely-dispersed parcels. Historians interpret this as a way of hedging climate risk.[8] Land in different locations would be affected differently by droughts, floods and frosts so by spreading land holdings over different locations, as well as by organizing agricultural cooperatives and buying insurance, farmers have succeeded in managing climate risk.

However, today's concerns about global climate change break new ground in two ways.[9] One is that the scope of potential damages is global. Climate changes will affect large numbers of people in the same way. A rise in sea level, for example, will affect low-lying coastal communities across the globe. The second is that climate change risks are driven by human activity. Unlike the risks associated with earthquakes or volcanic eruptions, which are beyond our ability to control, the risks of climate change are dependent upon our actions,[10] how fast and how extensively we are able to curb our emissions. Climate has always been unpredictable but the inclusion of these two new elements has magnified the degree of uncertainty significantly.

The risks of climate change are essentially unknowable in advance. Scientists have given us very good ideas about the types and severity of damages that we can expect from climate change. Yet we have no prior experience with systemic climate change from which we can infer the probability of future climate-related damages. Whereas it is possible to estimate a person's risk of contracting a disease because we have morbidity and mortality data to draw from, we have had no repeated experiments in climate change to guide us. Moreover, the damages at stake are potentially irreversible. The melting of the polar ice caps, species extinction and desertification, these are all processes that cannot be reversed, at least not on a human time scale. Waiting for greater certainty about climate change runs the risk of surpassing critical tipping thresholds from which there is no return.

With so much uncertainty about the expected damages from climate change, or alternatively, the anticipated benefits from climate change prevention, how can we estimate how much it is worth spending to stop global warming? We can't. There is no precise estimate, no magic number that will somehow resolve any concerns about whether climate policy makes good economic sense. The decision to invest in climate change prevention is not one that can be framed in simple cost–benefit terms. There is too much at stake, too much that is unknowable, too much that matters that economics can't appropriately account for and measure. Suffice to say that if the scientists are right about climate change and its consequences – and we have every reason to believe that they are – then it must make good economic sense to avoid it. The benefits of preserving the planet's climate system must outweigh the costs, even if we can't measure the benefits precisely. How could they not?

Can We Afford The Future?

This is the trillion dollar question at the heart of the climate debate. Solving climate change will be costly, so how costly is it and is it something we can afford?

How much it will cost to prevent climate change is something we can't really know in advance. The cost of preventing climate change will depend on how quickly we act; the longer we delay, the more we will have to reduce emissions in order to lower atmospheric carbon levels and the more costly it will be. If we are concerned about the costs of preventing climate change, stalling is definitely not the right strategy.

We also don't know how quickly new technologies will emerge and what those new technologies will look like. Until the creation of Kyoto's carbon market, which is still in its infancy, there was little incentive to reduce emissions, since no one had to pay for them. The carbon market, explained in more depth in Chapters 3 and 4, will reward those who reduce emissions and punish those who don't. This will spawn new technologies and new ways of doing business, no doubt. We're just not sure what they will be exactly.

We do have some estimates of what it may cost to prevent runaway climate change. These estimates should be taken with a grain of salt, but they at least give us some sense of what is at stake in the climate debate.[11] Recent studies suggest that countries may need to spend 1-3 per cent of their Gross Domestic Product (GDP) each year to stop rising greenhouse gas levels.[12] This means that 1-3 per cent of the value of what the world produces each year will have to be set aside to pay for emissions mitigation. In the scheme of things, this is not very much. But the costs are escalating as we speak. The longer we wait, the warmer the world will get, and the more we will have to spend to avoid the worst damages from climate change. In an influential report to the British government in 2006, former World Bank Chief Economist Sir Nicholas Stern estimated that that the world needs to spend 1 per cent of global GDP each year to protect the future from climate change. Stern warned that if we fail to slash carbon emissions soon, the world will suffer losses ranging from 5-20 per cent of global GDP each year. The longer we delay, the more likely it becomes that warming will surpass critical thresholds and the more devastating the losses will be.

For arguments sake, let us assume the highest cost scenario – that preventing climate change will cost as much as 3 per cent of global GDP per year. Is it worth it? Where you stand on this issue may partly depend on where you sit. In rich industrialized countries such as the US, the economy grows between 2-3 per cent a year in a typical year. Losing 3 per cent of GDP in any one year would mean that Americans would revert to the standard of living they had the previous year. This hardly signals a return to the Stone Ages. Had the US spent 3 per cent of its GDP on climate change in 2007, it would have cost $350 billion, or $1,170 per person.[13] No one will argue that these amounts are insignificant, but they are far less significant than they first appear. When turmoil in the financial markets led major US investment banks to collapse in September 2008, the US lost more than $400 billion in financial wealth in a 24-hour period. Poof – gone! To help remedy the financial crisis, the US spent more than $700 billion in its initial attempt to bail out cash-starved banks. The US will spend upwards of $1 trillion on the war in Iraq and Americans support the war in Iraq much less than they do climate change prevention.[14] The costs of protecting the future from climate damages may be well within the range of what most Americans are willing to pay.

In poor nations, losing 3 per cent of GDP is a much harder pill to swallow. This explains the reluctance of most poor nations to agree to binding limits on their greenhouse gas emissions. The key to saving the Kyoto Protocol will be finding ways to shield poor countries from the costs of preventing climate change. We'll explain more about how to do this in the chapters that follow.

Risks Too Great to Ignore

Now that we have some sense of what it may cost to prevent climate change, let us ask the question again. *Can we afford the future?*

, The truth is we can't afford not to. Whatever the exact costs of preventing climate change may be – 1 per cent or 3 per cent of global GDP – they pale in comparison to the potential costs of doing nothing. Failure to prevent climate change may cost the world as much as 20 per cent of global GDP each year.[15] The economic impacts of climate change may rival the Great Depression (the worldwide economic downturn originating in the US in 1929). What a terrible legacy to saddle our children and grandchildren with. Spending 1–3 per cent of global GDP to avoid damages as great as 5–20 per cent of global GDP is clearly well worth it if one is realistic about the alternatives – which are non-existent.

Consider some more evidence. According to a recent study, if climate change continues unchecked, the US will lose $1.9 trillion or 1.8 per cent of GDP each year from the combination of hurricane damages, residential property losses from sea-level rise, increased energy costs and water supply costs. Economy-wide impacts of global warming for the US may be as high as 3.6 per cent of GDP each year.[16] To put this number in context, the US economy grows by less than

Top 20 Cities Threatened by
Coastal Flooding From Climate Change *

Rank	Country	City	Potential Losses Today ($ billions)	Potential Losses 2070 ($ billions)
1	US	Miami	416	3,513
2	China	Guangzhou	84	3,358
3	US	New York–Newark	320	2,147
4	India	Calcutta	32	1,961
5	China	Shanghai	73	1,771
6	India	Mumbai	46	1,598
7	China	Tianjin	29	1,231
8	Japan	Tokyo	174	1,207
9	China	Hong Kong	36	1,164
10	Thailand	Bangkok	39	1,118
11	China	Ningbo	9	1,074
12	US	New Orleans	234	1,013
13	Japan	Osaka–Kobe	216	969
14	Netherlands	Amsterdam	128	844
15	Netherlands	Rotterdam	115	826
16	Vietnam	Ho Chi Minh City	27	653
17	Japan	Nagoya	110	623
18	China	Qingdao	3	602
19	US	Virginia Beach	85	582
20	Egypt	Alexandria	28	563

* cities ranked in terms of value of assets exposed to coastal flooding in 2070.
Source: Ranking of the World's Coastal Cities Most Exposed to Coastal Flooding Today and in The Future, OECD 2007.

3.6 per cent in most years. This means that the damages from climate change are significant enough to lower living standards.

Even more ominous is a recent study by the OECD. They estimated the economic damage that climate change could cause to major cities (see 'Top 20 Cities Threatened by Coastal Flooding From Climate Change' table on p36) by the year 2070. They predicted $3.5 trillion in property losses in Miami, $2.1 trillion in New York City, $1.9 trillion in Calcutta and $1.7 trillion in Shanghai. By 2070, 150 million people worldwide will be threatened by coastal flooding. The value of property lost to flooding alone could exceed $35 trillion.[17]

The human cost of climate change will be greater still. A recent World Health Organisation (WHO) study attributes more than 150 thousand deaths and five million illnesses each year to climate change.[18] A one metre (3ft) rise in sea level would submerge 2.2 sq km (0.8 sq mi) of land, mostly in Asia, displacing 145 million people at a global cost of $944 billion.[19] Alaska's towns are already sinking under the sea as its permafrost soil is melting; all of its towns are being relocated at a cost of $140,000 per Alaskan.[20] The ravages of hurricane Katrina in New Orleans gave the world a sobering glimpse of the magnitude of human suffering climate change might bring. More than 1,500 people died, 700 thousand people were evacuated, and hundreds of thousands of people have still not been able to return to their homes.

Swiss Re, the world's largest reinsurer, confirms an upward trend in the number, severity and costs of natural disasters. It reports that 14,600 people died worldwide from natural disasters in 2007, most of them in Asia and most of them because of storms and flooding. Bangladesh and India accounted for 6,700 of those who perished. Property losses from catastrophes in 2007 topped $70 billion. Most of this damage was not covered by insurance, although insurance companies worldwide did pay $23.3 billion in damages from natural disasters in 2007 and 84 per cent of insured losses worldwide in 2007 stemmed from natural disasters.[21] It is no wonder that insurance companies such as Swiss Re are calling on political leaders to find immediate solutions to the climate crisis.

Insurance for Future Generations

Reducing carbon emissions is like an insurance policy for future generations. It is a bet that we can't lose. Even if climate change ends up causing much less damage than scientists believe, reducing emissions will have led us to invest in new industries, develop new jobs and new technologies, and increase efficiency and productivity. If it causes damage on the scale now predicted, we will have saved lives and property.

In the face of such risks, public policy must find preventive measures. It is like insuring a house against fire. We are not sure it will happen but it is prudent to insure against such a loss. People routinely insure themselves against risks with much lower probabilities of occurrence than climate change. The chances of someone's house burning down or flooding are near zero; yet most people are willing to pay substantial amounts to insure their homes against these risks. Healthy young people who buy life insurance are another example. People routinely insure themselves against personal catastrophes that are much less likely than worse-case climate catastrophes for the planet. They are motivated by caution and a sense of responsibility to the loved ones they may leave behind. Their decisions account for the well-being of others alive today and others born in the future. Why shouldn't our decisions about climate change reflect the same prudence and commitment?

We should think of climate policy as an insurance policy against potentially catastrophic events. Our decisions should err on the side of caution. Compared with climate catastrophe, all other outcomes are irrelevant. And certainty regarding climate change impacts can only be achieved after it is too late.

If we treat emissions reduction as insurance for the planet and for future generations, the amount we need to spend to minimize the risks of catastrophic impacts makes perfect sense. The 'insurance premium' in this case is the cost of decreasing the carbon emissions that industrialized countries are mostly responsible for. According to the estimates we described above, we may need to spend 1–3 per cent

Worldwide Insurance Coverage in 2007 *

	Premiums ($ millions)	Growth (%)	World market share (%)	Premiums as a % of GDP	Premiums per capita ($)
North America	706,116	-1	42	4.6	2,115
Latin America and Caribbean	51,588	8	3	1.5	91
Europe	644,751	1	39	3.0	740
Western Europe	588,443	0	35	3.2	1,124
Central and Eastern Europe	56,308	12	3	2.1	173
Asia	706,116	5	13	1.6	54
Japan and industrialised Asian economies	147,187	2	9	2.4	687
South and East Asia	52,518	14	3	0.9	15
Middle East and Central Asia	17,427	10	1	1.1	57
Oceania	33,011	0	2	3.2	988
Africa	15,183	1	1	1.2	16
World	1,667,780	1	100	3.1	250
Industrialized countries	1,472,209	0	88	3.6	1,435
Emerging markets	195,571	10	12	1.3	34
OECD	1,481,257	0	89	3.5	1,209
G7	1,170,669	-1	70	3.7	1,556
EU, 15 countries	552,376	0	33	3.2	1,292
NAFTA	715,879	-1	43	4.4	1,626
ASEAN	14,370	6	1	1.0	25

* This includes coverage for man-made and natural disasters but not life insurance
Source: Swiss Re, Economic Research & Consulting, Sigma No. 3/2008.

of the world's GDP each year to minimize the risks of climate change. There is general agreement that such a 'premium' should be sufficient to avert the worst scenarios of climate change.

Spending 1–3 per cent of global GDP to reduce atmospheric carbon levels makes perfect sense from the insurance viewpoint. It is actually less than what the world currently pays to insure itself against catastrophes. Table 2.2 details what the world paid in 2007, a typical year, in premiums for all non-life insurance policies. This includes insurance policies to cover losses from natural disasters such as floods, fires and typhoons and man-made disasters such as plane crashes, rail disasters and shipwrecks.[22]

The table on p39 shows that, according to Swiss Re, the world already spends the equivalent of 3.1 per cent of global GDP, $250 per person, on insurance premiums to protect against human-made and natural disasters. Is it surprising to learn that the world already spends this much on insurance against low-probability but costly disasters? It could be. For years we have listened to opponents of the Kyoto Protocol tell us that the costs of preventing climate change, which are well within this range, are beyond what countries can reasonably afford.

North America spends 4.6 per cent of its GDP, $2,115 per person, on insurance policies to protect against risks that will be less damaging, on average, than climate change. Europe spends 3 per cent of its GDP, $740 per person, on insurance. What are Europeans and North Americans protecting themselves from? Why, disasters, of course! Natural disasters, including the floods, hurricanes, typhoons and droughts that climate change will increase the frequency and severity of, accounted for 42 per cent of all disasters in the world in 2007, 68 per cent of all deaths from disasters and 84 per cent of all insured losses in 2007.[23]

Certainly no one in the US, Canada or Europe refutes the logic of spending this much on disaster insurance each year. Why shouldn't we apply the same logic to climate change?

In terms of a return on investment, the premium to avoid climate change is a better bet. The world spent 3.1 per cent of global

GDP, $1.7 trillion, on non-life insurance premiums in 2007. Catastrophic damages that year amounted to just slightly more than one tenth of a percent of global GDP. And most of that damage was uninsured. Of the $70 billion in catastrophic damages, only $27.6 billion was insured.[24]

In comparison, the premium for averting catastrophic climate change is 1–3 per cent of global GDP. And at a minimum, we can avoid losses equivalent to 5 per cent of global GDP now and forever, according to the 2006 Stern Report.[25] If the worst predictions about climate change impacts are true, our insurance premium helps us to avoid damages as costly as 20 per cent of global GDP or more.

When individuals pay premiums for fire or flood insurance, they almost never see any of the money they paid come back to them. To insure against climate change, we pay today to avoid damages in the future. Our children and grandchildren will be the primary beneficiaries. But the premiums we pay to avoid future climate damages will also benefit us in the here and now. Here's why. In the US, for example, the energy-related sectors of the economy are not particularly 'labour-intensive'. This means that these sectors tend to employ more capital (machinery and equipment) than labour in production. Therefore money invested in the technologies and industries of the future could produce more jobs and money-making opportunities. Investments in energy efficiency will save households and businesses money on their energy bills and allow them to spend money on goods and services that can create more jobs compared with the jobs provided directly by the energy industry.

By all measures, insuring the future against catastrophic climate change is a prudent investment. The logic is so compelling there are only two possible reasons to deny it. Either we don't believe the science, or we discount the well-being of future generations. The science at this point seems compelling. Is it really that we care so little about the welfare of our grandchildren? Actions speak louder than words. It is long past time for action.

Who Pays for the Future?

Who should pay the premium for protecting future generations from climate change? As contentious as this question sounds, there is substantial agreement about the answer. The countries most responsible for the problem of climate change, the industrialized countries, should take the lead in global mitigation efforts. Not only are these countries to blame for two-thirds of global emissions, but their higher incomes mean that they are better able to afford emissions reduction than countries in Africa, Asia or Latin America where the majority of people survive on less than \$2 per day.[26]

To save the Kyoto Protocol as our insurance policy for the future we need to extend it beyond its 2012 deadline, find appropriate ways to limit emissions growth in developing countries and distribute most of the burden for paying for emissions reduction onto those who are most responsible. Sound impossible? It really isn't once we understand the role the global carbon market will play in reducing emissions and distributing the costs.

As we will see in Chapter 4, the most important thing the global carbon market does is attach a price to carbon emissions. Until recently, there was no cost associated with producing carbon emissions; therefore, there was no incentive to reduce them. The price of carbon in the global carbon market is expected to reach \$30 per tonne of carbon in the near future. The world currently produces the equivalent of 30 gigatonnes of carbon dioxide per year. If we require emission producers to pay for every tonne of emissions at a price of \$30 per tonne, it will generate \$900 billion dollars each year. This is equivalent to roughly 1 per cent of global GDP. Does this number sound familiar? It is similar to what it was estimated it would cost to avoid catastrophic climate change.

What does this mean? This means that using the carbon market to force emitters to pay for their emissions will generate enough income to offset the projected costs of preventing climate change. Remember how we agreed that it makes sense to pay a premium of at least 1 per cent of global GDP to insure against climate damages?

We now have a way to pay for it. The carbon market guarantees that the emitters will foot the bill. They will pay the premium for all of us.

It also means that the global economy will be no worse off for finally taking the threat of climate change seriously. By attaching a price to something that was previously treated as free – carbon emissions – the carbon market creates a new income source that can pay for emissions reductions. Emission producers will be the ones to pay for emission reductions. The carbon market allows us to shift the costs onto emission producers. The net cost to the global economy will be zero.

This sounds like an incredibly simple solution to a complex global problem. Unfortunately, saving Kyoto will not be quite so simple. The emitters understand well the implications to them of the carbon market and they stand ready to try and defeat it.

Short Term Solutions – Long Term Challenges

Fossil fuels create a Gordian knot of three key global issues: energy security, economic development and climate change. The fossil fuel age faces a cruel choice: economic development and energy independence clash against a stable climate. Today, we can't have them all. The attendant geopolitical conflicts take several forms. Fossil fuels are the primary energy source in the world today. Because they are unevenly distributed on the earth's crust they have led to wars and conflicts, prompting understandable calls for energy security and independence. At the same time economic development still depends crucially on the use of energy, and in today's economy, this means fossil fuels.

In the longer term, the only way out is to disentangle the use of energy from carbon emissions, namely make available clean and abundant renewable energy sources. But this is not feasible in the short term because of the sheer scale of the fossil infrastructure that must be replaced: about $40 trillion today, and with current trends about $400 trillion by the end of the century.[27] The short term and the long term present different problems, and require different solutions.

Time is not on our side. IPCC scientists agree that we need to stabilize or reduce carbon concentration in the atmosphere in the next 20 to 30 years. Avoiding further carbon emissions in no way solves the short-term problem. Even if we stabilize at the current level of emissions we still continue to add carbon dioxide to the atmosphere at a rate of 30 billion tonnes per year and therefore we will increase carbon concentration.

The solution for much of this problem is negative carbon – a type of technology, of which there are several, that is able to actually reduce carbon from the atmosphere in net terms. This is in contrast to technologies that simply reduce emissions, which at best leave the amount of carbon in the atmosphere unchanged. For instance, 'clean coal', that is achieving a great deal of attention in the US Congress and Senate, means coal that produces fewer or no emissions. The process of extracting that coal, however, is anything but clean.

Clean coal has a neutral 'footprint' in terms of emissions but at best it can leave atmospheric carbon unchanged. This may help as a stop-gap measure, if one forgets the other forms of environmental destruction that coal mining leaves in its wake. But even assuming this problem away for the moment, clean coal alone is not sufficient. New coal plants that clean the carbon they emit are a step forward but they create burdensome economic costs and, in any case, they merely stabilize the implacable growth of carbon concentration at current rates. More to the point, such coal plants defeat the long-term objective of making an orderly transition to non-fossil resources. It is critical that short-term goals be compatible with long-term objectives. We must avoid the trap of defeating long-term aims by focusing solely on short-term targets. Capturing carbon dioxide directly from fossil fuel power plants may delay the time of reckoning but it adversely impacts the long-term objective of replacing fossil fuels by renewable sources.

The long-term solution we seek is to disassociate energy use from fossil fuels. This cuts the Gordian knot referred to earlier, which ties energy use, economic development and climate change together. A long-term transition away from fossil fuels to alternative sources of energy[28] that are more broadly distributed can provide economic development and security without inducing global warming. A transition away from fossil fuel energy sources seems inevitable in the long term, because fossils are limited in supply. Alternative sources of energy are a necessary condition for sustainable development in the future and the rapidly growing world demand for energy will require a variety of alternative sources.[29] Supplies are not the problem. Solar, on its own, can easily meet a ten-fold increase using only 1 per cent of the energy that hits the planet's surface. And solar is democratically distributed on the planet. The sun shines its light on all nations.

However optimistic one may be for the long term, it is important to appreciate that this long-term solution is not appropriate for the short term. A transition to alternative energy sources is expected to take a long time since most of the energy used in the planet today is obtained from fossil fuels such as oil and coal.[30] As already pointed out, the change will take time and require a massive new and expensive infrastructure.[31] Yet as long as we continue to use fossil fuels and emit carbon we increase the concentration of greenhouse gases, and the risk of catastrophic climate change.[32]

So What's the Short-Term Solution?

In reality, we cannot eliminate fossil fuels from our economy overnight. A quick and drastic reduction in emissions is not feasible due to the sheer size of the fossil infrastructure that needs to be replaced.[33] Indeed, rich and poor nations could be seriously affected by economic disruptions caused by a drastic decrease in the use of fossil fuels. Rapidly growing nations such as China and India are heavily dependent on coal; so is the US and Russia. Hydroelectric power is only 6 per cent of world energy use, about the same as nuclear power, and renewable sources account for only 1 per cent of the world's energy production today. It does not seem realistic to drastically decrease the use of fossil fuels in the short term, which is why there is an increasing call to capture the carbon emitted by fossil fuels plants and store it safely.

Since we focus on the long term, we take into consideration that the alternative source should be able to provide five to ten times the energy used in the world today. This is a standard projection of energy demand by the end of this century.[34] None of the five main types of renewable energy – hydroelectric, geothermal, solar, wind and biomass resources – nor nuclear energy can offer this possibility, either because they lack the capacity or because to do so would create additional problems. For example, biomass for energy competes with food production, and is much less efficient per square metre than solar (about 3 per cent of the energy potential provided by solar for the same surface area) and hydroelectric lacks the capacity and has environmental consequences. But solar energy – in particular Concentrated Solar Power (CSP) – could easily meet the demand with limited environmental impact. A combination of all of these energy sources that includes solar could therefore offer a reasonable long-term solution.

In the short term, about 10 years, we need negative carbon. This implies a way of reducing the atmospheric concentration of carbon altogether. The technology strategy should accommodate both the short- and long-term goals, and the transition of the short into the long term. This is a tall order because such a technology must simultaneously facilitate the transition to alternative sources providing for massive increases in supplies for the long term, while in the short term allow the continued use of fossil fuels and simultaneously decrease the carbon content in the planet's atmosphere.

Among several available technologies, one called the Global Thermostat – introduced by Chichilnisky and Eisenberger – has the capability to produce electricity while simultaneously decreasing carbon in the atmosphere by air-extraction and storage (cogeneration of electricity and carbon capture).[35] In this process, the carbon concentration in the atmosphere decreases while producing electrical power. This patent-pending process uses the residual process heat that remains after the production of electricity to capture carbon from the atmosphere. Electricity is produced by turbines driven with high heat – about 300°C (570°F) – and after the high heat is used, the residual low process heat can be used to capture carbon from air. This process uses any source of process heat to cogenerate electricity and carbon capture (fossil fuels, nuclear or concentrated solar power plants, aluminum smelters, refineries and others) and can make a fossil fuel power plant a 'net carbon sink', namely a site that actually reduces atmospheric carbon.[36] Such a combination is unusual and contrasts with the physical realities of the fossil fuel economy, where the more energy that is produced the more carbon dioxide is emitted. The technology proposed has the property that the more electricity power it produces, the more it reduces the carbon content in the atmosphere. This provides real protection against human-induced climate change since it allows us to become carbon neutral in the short term, and enables an orderly transition from the short term to a renewable energy future, enhancing energy security and economic development.

As we will see in the chapters that follow, the Kyoto Protocol ensures that developing countries can be compensated for emissions reductions that take place within their borders. Rich countries can purchase certified carbon offsets from developing countries through Kyoto's Clean Development Mechanism (CDM) and apply them towards their own emission targets. Negative carbon technologies could provide more financial compensation for developing nations through the CDM than simply stabilizing emissions. Global Thermostat plants would get credit both for the avoided carbon from using a carbon neutral source of energy to produce electricity and for the reduction in carbon dioxide that they provide through air capture and storage. Thus, the CDM can be a powerful tool in the financing of Global Thermostat Plants in developing nations. This in turn can provide developing nations in the long term with clean energy infrastructure, and in the short term it can provide transfer of technology and a source of clean and abundant energy to grow their economies.[37] This is just one example.

Even more important, however, is the fact that this type of technology can help level the playing field between poor countries while reducing the risks to all countries from climate change. The recent investment boom in poor countries resulting from the Kyoto Protocol's CDM has benefited some poor countries much more than others. Investments are now flowing into China to build hydroelectric, wind power and, most recently, natural gas-fired power plants. Why China? Simple. This is where most of the developing world's emissions are coming from. Indeed, 18 per cent of world emissions come from China, while only 3 per cent come from the entire African continent. This is natural in a nation that by itself represents 20 per cent of the world population. But there are some inequities in a programme that encourages 60 per cent of all CDMs to fund changes in China's energy structure, while leaving out the poorest nations in the world because they happen to emit so little. This problem can and should be corrected.

Africa plays a lesser role in Kyoto's current CDM. It receives little today in the way of technology and wealth transfers under Kyoto because it consumes so little energy and generates too few emissions. Today, the Kyoto Protocol and the CDM are all about reducing emissions – period. And since so little reduction can be achieved in Latin America or in Africa there is little role for them to play.

But all this changes with negative carbon technologies. These could be located in Africa or in Latin America and could allow those regions to play a significant role in global climate change prevention efforts. With negative carbon, Africa could significantly reduce carbon in the atmosphere, therefore becoming an excellent candidate for CDM projects, perhaps even a better one than China. Will this happen? Will Africa be able to capture 30 per cent of the world carbon even though it emits only 3 per cent. Can Africa save the world? To answer this, we must first explore the Kyoto Protocol, its carbon market and its CDM.

The Road to Kyoto

3

The Kyoto Protocol is not the final solution to the climate crisis. It is a start, an initial attempt towards resolving global warming. Yet it contains the seed for a global solution to the worst global environmental issue we face today – climate change – and perhaps to others as well. The Protocol was designed to be a first step, an experiment in how to reduce greenhouse gas emissions around the world by international agreement. It indicates the way forward rather than the end of the path. The provisions of the Kyoto Protocol expire in 2012 in their own terms and by deliberate design.

The 1997 Kyoto Protocol took a long time to emerge and was the culmination of a long and contested process of information gathering and diplomatic negotiations for the nations of the world. The drama continues today. Not even the Treaty of Versailles, which ended World War I, or the Bretton Woods system, which rebuilt the world's war-torn financial system in 1944, were as long, complex and difficult to negotiate as the Kyoto Protocol.

The history of the Kyoto Protocol is fascinating. It contains many elements of a blockbuster Hollywood film – suspense, drama, intrigue – and it is easy to lose sight of the seriousness of what is at stake. If climate disaster strikes in this story it won't end because the cinema lights pop on and the credits start to roll. Indeed the Kyoto Protocol, the only international agreement we have for dealing with the potentially catastrophic risks of climate change, is itself at risk today. It may well collapse before it expires in 2012.

Two factors stall the current negotiations: the position of the US and the position of developing nations such as India and China. So far, the US has refused to ratify and comply with the Kyoto Protocol. This is, in part, because developing nations such as China, which currently produces 18 per cent of the world's emissions but houses 1.3 billion people, could become the major greenhouse gas emitters of the future. Yet under the 1992 United Nations Climate Convention, neither China nor India is obliged to curtail its emissions. The US views this as a major stumbling block to achieving sustainable emission reductions, something that could undermine its own emissions reduction efforts. Behind this, there are also fears of unfair advantage and competition for global leadership. China is the US's major global economic rival, following a decade in which China's economy expanded at a phenomenal 10 per cent growth rate each year. Since the Kyoto Protocol was initially designed and voted on in 1997, China has become a major economic power.

Developing nations, on the other hand, view any demands on them to curtail emissions as unfair, since they only emit 40 per cent of the global emissions today while they house over 80 per cent of the world's population. At present, developing nations are not only more frugal in their use of the planet's atmosphere than the industrial nations – as indicated by their vastly lower emissions – but they also use energy more efficiently in terms of gross domestic product (GDP). GDP is so tied to energy use that reducing emissions means reducing economic growth, as the graph on p51, 'GDP and Carbon Emissions' illustrates.

Since the climate crisis cannot be solved without all nations reducing carbon emissions, it is clear that the current impasse in global negotiations must be solved. The solution must include a clear timetable for a commitment from the developing nations to reduce emissions under some set of acceptable circumstances, in the future. But we may be getting ahead of the story. To understand the current situation we must start from the beginning. How did it all start?

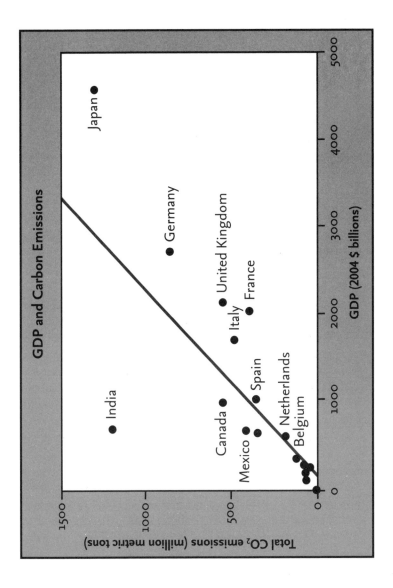

GDP and Carbon Emissions

Total CO$_2$ emissions (million metric tons)

GDP (2004 $ billions)

Japan

Germany

United Kingdom

France

Italy

Spain

Netherlands

Belgium

India

Canada

Mexico

51

An Insider's Timeline of the Kyoto Protocol

Graciela Chichilnisky was the architect of the Kyoto Protocol's global carbon market. She offers the following history and personal account of the Protocol.

Climatology was once a small and obscure branch of science. Yet important discoveries made in the 19th century made it one of the most important fields of scientific study in the world. Listed below are some key dates in climate change history, and my personal account of the creation of the carbon market of the Kyoto Protocol. At present, negotiators from 180 countries are attempting to draft a plan to solve global warming that will begin where Kyoto leaves off in 2012.

The Scientific Basis is Laid

In **1824** the French physicist Joseph Fourier is the first to describe a 'greenhouse effect' in a paper delivered to Paris's Académie Royale des Sciences.

In **1861** Irish physicist John Tyndall carries out research on radiant heat and the absorption of radiation by gases and vapours including carbon dioxide and water. He shows that carbon dioxide changes the atmosphere quality so that the atmosphere admits the entrance of solar heat but checks its exit. The result is a tendency to accumulate heat at the surface of the planet.[1]

In **1896** Swedish chemist Svante Arrhenius first proposes the idea of a man-made greenhouse effect. He hypothesizes that the increase in the burning of coal since the beginning of industrialization could lead to an increase in atmospheric carbon dioxide and heat up the earth. Arrhenius was trying to find out why the earth experienced ice ages. He thought the prospect of future generations living 'under a milder sky' would be a desirable state of affairs.

In **1938** British engineer Guy Stewart Callendar compiles temperature statistics in a variety of regions and finds that over the previous century the mean temperature had risen markedly. He also discovers that carbon dioxide levels have risen 10 percent during the same period. He concludes that carbon dioxide is the most likely reason for the rise in temperature.

In **1955** John Hopkins University researcher Gilbert Plass proves that increased levels of carbon dioxide could raise atmospheric temperature. (By 1959 Plass is boldly predicting that the earth's temperature will rise more than 16°C [28.8°F] by the end of the century.) In the same year chemist Hans Suess detects the fossil carbon produced by burning fuels. Although he and Roger Revelle, director of the Scripps Institute of Oceanography, declare that the oceans must be absorbing the majority of atmospheric carbon dioxide, they decide to conduct further research.

In **1957,** a seminal article by Revelle and Seuss reports 'Humans are now carrying on a large-scale geophysical experiment'. In **1958** Revelle and Suess employ geochemist Charles Keeling to continuously monitor carbon dioxide levels in the atmosphere. After only two years of measurements in Antarctica an increase is visible. The graph becomes widely known as the Keeling Curve and becomes an icon of global warming debate and continues to chart the year on year rise in carbon dioxide concentrations to this day.

By **1963** the Conservation Foundation reports 'It is estimated that a doubling of the carbon dioxide content of the atmosphere would produce a temperature rise of 3.8°C (6.84°F).'

In **1979** NASA reports 'There is no reason to doubt that climate change will result from human carbon dioxide emissions, and no reason to believe that these changes will be negligible.' Notice that this was almost 30 years ago and yet the problem is still with us today.

Climate Change as a Global Concern Emerges

In **1979** the first International Conference on Climate Change takes place; it involves mostly scientists. The First World Climate Conference introduces the threat of climate change to the global community and calls on the nations of the world to anticipate and guard against potential climate hazards. The World Climate Programme is established at this meeting. This is the first of many international conferences on climate change.

Political interest in climate change peaks after the **1985** Villach meeting in Austria, at which scientists at the World Climate Programme conference confidently predict that increased carbon dioxide concentrations will lead to a significant rise in the mean surface temperatures of the earth.

That same year, a hole in the ozone layer is discovered over Antarctica. It provides further evidence that human economic activity is altering the planet in dangerous ways. A heat wave in North America in **1987**, the hottest year on record to date, adds a direct experience of the possible changes envisioned. Three years later, the 1980s would officially become the hottest decade on record. The 1987 Brundtland Commission famous report 'Our Common Future', which introduces the concept of sustainable development to the international community, adds further fuel to the emerging climate debate.

The political agenda develops rapidly after two 1987 workshops sponsored by the Beijer Institute in Vilach and Bellagio. It becomes clear that in order to address the climate problem, the scientific issues have to be clarified first. This is achieved by an interdisciplinary group of scientists across the world that includes physicists, atmospheric scientists, biologists and economists, all working as part of the Intergovernmental Panel on Climate Change (IPCC), which is set up in 1988 by the World Meteorological Organization (WMO) and by the United Nations Environment Programme (UNEP). The IPCC provides reports based on scientific evidence that are widely regarded as reflecting the dominant viewpoints of the global scientific community.

In **1988** a drought in the US reduces parts of the Mississippi River to a trickle and sets much of Yellowstone National Park ablaze. This further kindles public interest in the possibility of climate change. In June, Dr James Hansen of the NASA Goddard Institute for Space Studies at Columbia University delivers his testimony to the US Senate. Based on computer models and temperature measurements he states that he is 99 per cent sure that the greenhouse effect has been detected and it is already changing the climate.

In **1989** the Second World Climate Conference is held in Geneva, only this time it includes representatives from countries worldwide as well as members of the scientific community. It is this conference that lays the groundwork for the current international climate regime by calling for the creation of an international convention on climate change. The United Nations soon establishes a committee to negotiate the convention text. It eventually becomes the United Nations Framework Convention on Climate Change (UNFCCC), the international body charged with the clarification, negotiation and resolution of climate change. Not only is the UNFCCC notable as one of the first major international environmental agreements, but it firmly embraces the notions of sustainable development and shared responsibility for the health of the planet.

In **1990** the IPCC delivers its first assessment on the state of climate change, predicting an increase of 0.3°C (0.54°F) each decade in the 21st century, greater than any rise seen over the previous 10 thousand years. This report is influential in shifting pubic opinion in favour of the seriousness of climate change.

International Negotiation Begins in Earnest

In **1992** The United Nations Conference on Environment and Development, better known as the Earth Summit, takes place in Rio de Janeiro. It is attended by 172 countries. One hundred and fifty nations agree that the international community should focus on efforts towards 'sustainable development', which are defined as those policies that satisfy the basic needs of the present without undermining the rights of future generations to satisfy their needs; I had introduced the concept of basic needs as part of the Bariloche Latin American World Economic Model in 1977.[2]

The Earth Summit marks the first unified global effort to come to grips with global warming. Most notably, the UNFCCC is signed by 154 nations at the Earth Summit. Negotiations that take place at the Earth Summit eventually lead to the 1997 Kyoto Protocol.

Today, the UNFCCC enjoys near universal membership. More than 190 countries have ratified it. Within the Climate Convention, the Conference of the Parties to the Convention (COP) plays the most important role. The COP is responsible for meeting and making the necessary decisions to implement the UNFCCC's objective. That objective is to stabilize greenhouse gas concentrations so as to prevent dangerous interference with the climate system and enable economic development to proceed in a sustainable manner.[3]

The UNFCCC affirms the global community's intent to preserve the climate system for present and future generations and set forth the principles of cooperation between states. It establishes the precautionary principle as the defining reason for global action to prevent climate change. It recommends the creation of cost-effective mechanisms for achieving emissions reduction, consistent with sustainable development and designed to provide 'no regrets' safeguards against such risks. These steps should also be compatible with food security, social justice and the wealth of nations.[4]

Most importantly, Article 4 of the UNFCCC establishes the notion of common but differentiated responsibilities for mitigating climate change on the basis of countries' contributions to the build-up of greenhouse gas concentrations in the past and their ability to afford reductions in the present. As we will see, it is this principle, founded in the spirit of fairness and partnership, that leads to serious conflict between industrialized and developed countries over whether and how to cap developing country emissions. It is this conflict, more so than any other, that threatens the future of the Kyoto Protocol.

Article 4 of the 1992 UNFCCC assures that industrial nations take the lead in emissions reduction and that developing nations will not be asked to reduce their emissions without compensation. All countries that participate in the UN Climate Convention have certain obligations. They must all provide greenhouse gas inventories, national strategies and measures and reports. The UNFCCC encourages industrial nations to reduce their emissions and to provide financial assistance to developing nations to achieve the conventions' goals.

But very soon after the UN framework convention is completed it becomes clear that most countries are not on track to meet their non-binding emissions aims. It is evident that a new agreement has to be negotiated.

It seems worth stepping back for a moment to summarize how global climate negotiations operate, if for no other reason than to illustrate how international change processes unfold, how difficult it is to gain consensus and how necessary global cooperation is to achieving a solution. Through the use of framework conventions and protocols, the approach is to allow states to proceed incrementally; a framework convention establishes a system of governance, and specific obligations are developed in protocols. After the 1992 Earth Summit, the UNFCCC is created to establish a general system of international governance for climate-related issues. To build scientific consensus step by step as well, the work of the UNFCCC is based on the IPCC, the scientific body that includes thousands of scientists from all participating nations. The IPCC confirms the human origins of climate change in its second assessment report in 1995. Through the work of the UNFCCC, on 11 December 1997, 160 countries vote in favour of the Kyoto Protocol. But we are getting ahead of the story...

Between the Earth Summit in 1992 and the creation of the Kyoto Protocol in 1997, several notable events occur. First, the UNFCCC enters into force in March of **1994** and the COP becomes its ultimate authority. The COP convenes its first meeting in Berlin in **1995**. The IPCC, the scientific advisory board to the UNFCCC, completes its second assessment report in 1995 just in time for the second COP meeting in Geneva. This report issues the first official statement confirming humans' impact on the global climate, finding a 'discernable effect of human carbon emissions on the earth's climate.' As if to drive home the message, temperatures around the world soar to record highs in 1995. The 1990s soon replaces the 1980s as the hottest decade on record. There is no longer much doubt that climate change is a real risk with a human cause. Public opinion worldwide wakes up to the realities of climate change and demands solutions.

The Road to Kyoto

Emphasis Shifts from Science to Economics

By the early 1990s, the international community realizes that the key to resolving the physical problem of climate change lies in social organization, in particular, in economics. The causes of climate change are economic, steeped in the ways we use energy to produce goods and services in the world economy, while the effects are best measured and understood by the physical sciences. As scientific consensus begins to emerge about the human causes of climate change and its possible effects, the emphasis shifts from the science of climate change to the economics. This complicates the problem enormously, as these are two disciplines that rarely communicated before. The effects of climate change are physical; therefore economists are at odds to measure them. Yet the causes of climate change are economic; therefore there is little or nothing that physicists can do to resolve the problem on their own. The IPCC realizes that it needs to enlarge its work by including economists. It is about this time that I start collaborating with the IPCC, and by **1997** I become a lead author of the IPCC, representing the US.

The increasing emphasis on economic issues also leads to the recognition that a crucial aspect of the problem lies in the relationship between rich and poor nations and that while most of the emissions originated historically from the rich nations, in the future the developing nations could become the largest emitters in the world. The concentration of carbon in the atmosphere of the planet is the same for all nations. Each nation can inflict damage on the rest by emitting carbon. Therefore, all nations have to agree to reduce emissions. Collaboration between the rich and the poor nations becomes central to resolving the climate problem. But it is a thorny issue, since developing nations need energy to develop and industrial nations worry that growing energy demands in the developing world will further fuel global warming. Without collaboration between the two groups of countries there can be no solution.

In June **1993** the Organization of Economic Cooperation and Development (OECD), an international organization that represents the rich nations of the world, hosts an international conference at their offices in Paris, France, in which the major players in the global climate negotiations explore the connection between global warming and the economy. (In retrospect, this conference laid the groundwork for the framework of the Kyoto Protocol in 1997.) The conference includes the Economics Division of the OECD, the department where the economists Peter Sturm and Joaquim Oliveira Martins work. It includes representatives from industrial and developing nations, in recognition of the need to involve all nations in the resolution. One of the speakers is Ambassador Raul Estrada Oyuela, who later becomes the lead negotiator of the Kyoto Protocol. Another participant is Jean-Charles Hourcade, who becomes part of the French delegation to the UNFCCC, and who later invites me to write the crucial wording introducing the carbon market into the Protocol.

In my presentation at this conference I propose the creation of the carbon market that eventually becomes an essential part of the Kyoto Protocol. I explain the value of the market approach and the need for preferential treatment for developing nations, effectively establishing the connection between equity and efficiency in carbon markets: the carbon market has the potential to become an effective way to promote efficient allocations of resources in the economy (efficiency), encouraging clean technologies, while at the same time reducing the inequalities of income and consumption throughout the world economy (equity). The proposal I presented at the 1993 OECD meeting eventually becomes the foundation for the creation of the carbon market and the Clean Development Mechanism (CDM) of the Kyoto Protocol. But at this point in time, my presentation is quite controversial and leads to much debate. Raul Estrada Oyuela, who represents Argentina in the global negotiations, is against the use of markets in environmental conservation, as is Peter Sturm, who opposes the results linking equity and efficiency in carbon markets. Most European economists at the time are against the market approach and prefer carbon taxes. The debate on carbon markets arising from this conference grows surprisingly large, and involves economists and diplomats across Europe, the US and Latin America. I publish several articles and books showing, for the first time, that in economic terms carbon concentration is really a public good and therefore, its properties are quite different from standard private goods. In particular, I show that with global public goods, it is impossible to separate efficiency concerns from equity concerns.

The Controversy Grows...

At this time, almost everyone believes that the majority of the abatement of carbon emissions should be done in developing nations, based on the assumption that the costs would be lower. Economist Larry Summers had famously argued in an internal World Bank memo that developing nations should be sent the pollution from rich nations, as it would be more cost efficient for them to clean the pollution. Geoffrey Heal and I then publish an article in *Economic Letters* in 1994 showing exactly the opposite, namely that abatement should be done mostly by industrialized nations, that it is more efficient if rich nations abate their own emissions even if it costs more. This fuels the controversy further since the conventional wisdom that applies to private goods, but not to public goods, dictates the opposite.

As the controversy grows on both sides of the Atlantic, my research and my proposal for a global carbon market become a well-known source of scientific debate. The OECD starts to recognize the diplomatic and economic importance of the issues involved and I become a consultant, writing a report on carbon markets for the OECD Economics Division with Geoffrey Heal.5 I also continue working as an adviser to various UN organizations and to the World Bank, as I had done since the mid 1970s. In that role I build with Professor Geoffrey Heal at Columbia University a version of the OECD Green Model of the world economy and enlarge it to include a carbon market. This becomes the first model of the global economy that simulates the behaviour of the global carbon market. I publish the results in a book produced under the auspices of the United Nations entitled, *Development and Global Finance: The Case for* an International Bank for Environmental Settlements.[6] These results show the efficiency advantages of assigning the poor nations more rights than rich nations to produce greenhouse gases.

In **1995** I publish the OECD Report no. 153, 'Markets for Tradeable CO_2 Emission Quotas: Principles and Practice' with Geoffrey Heal, then at Columbia Business School. It introduces, for the first time, the idea of the global carbon market to a major international organization led by industrial nations, the OECD. We explain how the global carbon market could operate in practice. This is the beginning of the carbon market's public role in Europe. We also explain the advantage of markets over taxes for reducing global emissions (see Chapter 4).

The controversy arising from my OECD presentation and the OECD report that we produced continues growing and includes Peter Sturm of the Economics Division of the OECD, and other distinguished economists in the US such as David Starrett, who was then the Chairman of the Economics Department at Stanford University. Geoffrey Heal and I write a joint paper with David Starrett on the basic economic structure of the global carbon market, laying down the rationale for a preferential role for the developing nations. Peter Sturm and Joaquim Oliveira Martins write a piece explaining their differing position on the matter, which eventually is clarified and attributed to their assumption that environmental quality is not a factor of economic welfare. Geoffrey Heal and I decide to memorialize the entire debate, warts and all, in a book that is published in 2000 by Columbia University Press, *Environmental Markets: Equity and Efficiency*.

During 1994 and 1995 I continue presenting my case for a carbon market proposal in many universities in the Americas, Europe, Asia and Australia, at the US Senate and in US Congress. My case has two parts. The first part argues for the market because it starts by requiring global emission limits nation by nation. The second part, which has to do with 'equity', recognizes that the fact that, since carbon concentration in the atmosphere is a global public good, this requires a measure of equity in the treatment of the poor nations.

The first part was congenial to mainstream economists in industrial nations, while the second was attractive to environmentalists and politicians from developing nations. While market efficiency was never debated, the role of equity in attaining efficiency was the source of a continued uphill debate. There was some degree of sympathy with giving a preferential role to poor nations, but always as a matter of charity or good will and not as a matter of securing efficiency. The reality is that the global carbon market trades a very different type of good, a global public good, and is therefore a different market from any other seen in the world until now. This leads to a new type of economics, something that is discussed below.

As time passes, I press my market approach in academic and political publications and even in newspapers and magazine articles and on TV. In 1994 I publish an article in the *American Economic Review* (AER), 'North–South Trade and the Global Environment', showing how the global warming problem and the global poverty problem are one and the same. Both derive from excessive exports of natural resources by developing nations. Developing nations do not export natural resources because of comparative advantages. More often than not they over-extract and export natural resources because they lack private property rights over those resources. Resources in developing nations are often treated as common property and used on a first come, first served basis. As I showed in the 1994 AER publication, this leads directly to a global tragedy of the commons: overexploitation of resources in the South (developing countries) and overconsumption in the North (developed countries). I explain in this article how the excessive emphasis on resource exports, such as petroleum, damages the economy of developing nations and undermines their ability to develop, grow and feed their people. The Kyoto Protocol carbon market corrects all this: it creates property rights on the use of global commons, resolving the tragedy of the commons. These results were considered almost heretical at a time when most economists were espousing the then popular theory of 'export-led growth'. Now the results are widely accepted and often considered evident.

At the same time, I argue for the equity features that need to be included in global carbon markets as an advisor to the US government, various United Nations organizations and as a lead author of the IPCC. My article with Professor Heal in *Economic Letters* presents the scientific case for a link between equity and efficiency in these markets, as does our OECD 1995 report and the Pegram Lectures I give later at the Brookhaven National Laboratories in Long Island, New York, in 1999.[7] The equity efficiency link in global carbon markets becomes my trademark, and a continued source of debate on both sides of the Atlantic and in international organizations.

To drive the point home and show how the carbon market would operate, I develop, with Geoffrey Heal and Yun Lin, a computerized model of a world economy that includes a global carbon market at the Program on Information and Resources (PIR/Green) at Columbia University. This new global model extends the earlier OECD GREEN global model. It introduces a market for emissions trading and shows in practical terms the positive impacts that a global carbon market can have on the global environment and on the world economy.

The empirical model is useful in helping people visualize the creation of the new global carbon market and how it would operate. This is the first time a global economy is seen functioning with a global carbon market and the benefits become apparent. I present results in the US Congress and at several UN meetings. The results show that policies that benefit developing nations – for example, mixed allocations of permits that include population as well as GDP as a basis for the allocation – were more efficient than those that simply considered GDP. 'Grandfathering' (awarding emissions rights to nations according to their own historic pattern of emissions) is, in fact, less efficient than providing more allocations to the poor nations.[8]

The global model validates the value of allocating more emission rights to developing nations and explains how this would work in practice. This anticipates the allocation of emission rights that eventually prevails in the Kyoto Protocol in 1997. Our model becomes useful to validating this approach and making it happen.

Kyoto Begins to Take Form

Until the mid 1990s the public is still unconvinced of the risks of climate change; the issue is still widely disbelieved and misunderstood. However, by **1995**, the hottest year on record, the discourse begins to shift. The second IPCC Assessment that year states for the first time that 'the balance of evidence suggests a discernible human influence on global climate.' This is the first scientific assessment that gives an unequivocal signal that the earth's climate is changing and its changes are, on balance, due to human causes. The international political response is to take the issue of climate change more seriously and to seek global solutions.

In December 1996 I am invited to give the Key Note speech at the Annual Meeting of the World Bank in Washington DC. I officially propose the creation of a global carbon market, explaining why this solution would be superior to carbon taxes and how this approach could favour the industrial and developing nations. This presentation is attended by hundreds of people and it becomes the first official US proposal for the carbon market and its CDM.

In 1996 the UNFCCC Convention of the Parties meets in Berlin and agrees on the so-called Berlin Mandate, which is, one might say, an 'agreement to agree'. This Mandate requires UN negotiators to come up with a solution to the climate change issue by the next COP meeting in Kyoto 1997. Ambassador Raul Estrada Oyuela is elected as the lead negotiator for the negotiations in Kyoto, and he inherits this same mandate: to reach an agreement at the next COP. As a professional diplomat, Raul takes this mandate very seriously, and he is determined to reach an agreement in Kyoto. The task is enormous, since industrial and developing nations are now more divided than ever on the climate change issue.

Believing that the only way to reach an agreement is to find a solution that appeals to both industrial and developing nations, I continue to press my case in favour of the carbon market in presentations and publications around the world. My proposal for a global market approach protects developing nations and elicits a favourable response from the US, which supports market approaches. Any proposal that has the simultaneous approval of the industrial and the developing nations is a very good start, since the most thorny aspect of the climate negotiations is the tug of war between the rich and the poor nations.

I label my global carbon market proposal as a two-sided coin because it offers a market solution that attracts the industrial nations concerns for efficiency and flexibility, while simultaneously offering developing nations an 'equity' approach through the allocation of the rights to emit that appeals to their own concerns for poverty alleviation and historical fairness. My own view in debating with the US and developing nations' representatives is that the positions of the North and the South are so diametrically opposed that only a solution that appears opposite to each side will prevail. My proposal for a global carbon market truly looks opposite to each side.

However, in all candour, my carbon market approach is not popular at the time. In fact for many years it is opposed by all sides. Neither developing nations, environmentalists nor industrial nations favour it. Academics are also surprised or antagonized to hear my arguments that a global carbon market would blend equity with efficiency; they are rather skeptical of such properties in a market. At the time I am a Trustee of the Natural Resources Defense Council where Robert Kennedy Jr, the son of President Kennedy's brother, is an environmental attorney. On two occasions I debate the issue with Robert Kennedy Jr at the Reuters Forum on TV; his telegenic anti-market environmentalism always wins while my rational pro-carbon market approach is a loser, at least in emotional terms with the audience. His argument is simple: the market is the enemy of the environment so how can we enlist the market to solve the largest environmental problem of our times?

Robert Kennedy Jr is not alone at the time. Raul Estrada Oyuela, a great environmentalist who had become a collaborator in conferences and writings since the 1993 OECD meeting, is still also set against the carbon market. This is more serious. Indeed, none of the environmentalists I know at this point are in favour of the carbon market – for them the idea is like trying to buy or sell your own grandmother – physically possible but morally repugnant.

It will take all of my 20 years of credibility as a developing nation supporter and as the creator of the concept of basic needs to get developing nations to support the idea. My explanation that the carbon market is different from all other markets because of the public good aspects of atmospheric carbon dioxide, which induces an equity principle in the way emission limits are assigned, is somewhat helpful. But it is a hard sell, as it is a difficult concept to comprehend. In reality, the carbon market, because it trades a global public good, is very different from all other markets we know. It is a unique market in history.

The Europeans in the OECD are also dead set against the carbon market in 1997. Their approach is closely aligned with carbon taxes. The late James Tobin, a great US economist and a Nobel Laureate from Yale University, publicizes his proposal for a general approach to globalization, based on creating a global carbon tax for reducing carbon emissions. His overall proposal is called 'The Tobin Tax'. Neither the North nor the South, nor most of my own fellow academics, are on my side in this debate. Once again, just as it was when I defined basic needs, I find myself arguing against the mainstream establishment. This time I have to argue against mainstream environmentalists as well.

Arguing My Case

Moreover, the tables are all turned in this debate. The whole thing is a bit paradoxical. I'm advocating a market solution, the global carbon market, which opposes the tax approach that is popular at the time within the industrial nations, the US and the OECD as a whole. In doing so, I oppose James Tobin, who is well known and liked, who advocates a global tax on carbon, while I, representing the side of fairness for developing nations, am advocating a free market approach. This paradox is more an illusion than a fact. The carbon market starts from setting firm ceilings on emissions and therefore it is closer to the heart of an environmentalist than a carbon tax that has no certain impact on the quantities emitted. It allows each nation to use their own internal approach, such as limits, markets and taxes. Eventually, despite the almost universal feeling that markets favour industrial nations and are dangerous for the environment, I am somehow able to turn the tables and show that the environment and the developing nations will benefit more from the carbon market than from using carbon taxes (for more on why this is, see pp84–88).

In 1997, in addition to the unending academic and UN debates, I present my proposals through the US Undersecretary of State, Timothy Wirth, to experts in the US Department of State and through the US Under Secretary of the Treasury, Larry Summers, to experts in the US Department of the Treasury. Both Wirth and Summers are interested and supportive. I could say they are my natural public, possibly the only natural public and allies I have in all this. However, I have a suspicion that they could be supporting my ideas for the wrong reasons. They do not seem to understand, nor do they appear to care much, about the 'equity' piece of the carbon market that is so important to me, and, of course, to developing nations. Indeed, the debate on this North–South equity issue in the carbon market still continues today.

Yet eventually the two-sided coin argument prevails. The attractiveness of the market approach wins the day in the US. I agitate in every possible way I can, including in the US Congress and Senate, where I receive interested, if diffused, attention. In the process I meet with US Vice President Al Gore, a very intelligent man with a very positive agenda but not inherently given to market approaches.

I organize special meetings at Columbia University with the negotiators of the Kyoto Protocol, to explain the somewhat counterintuitive fact that the market approach will benefit the developing nations of the world. In the autumn of 1996, Peter Eisenberger creates the Earth Institute at Columbia University, based on the research agenda of the Program on Information and Resources

(PIR) that I founded and have directed since 1994. Eisenberger views my efforts as the cornerstone of the research agenda on globalization at Columbia University, which of course, they are. PIR starts a close cooperation with the Earth Institute, which joins forces with my proposal for a global carbon market. This strategic alliance between the Earth Institute and my centre PIR proves very productive, and becomes a crucial step in the road to Kyoto.

In April 1997 I publish the UN book, *Development and Global Finance*, exploring how the carbon market works and how the same market approach can solve other environmental issues such as biodiversity destruction. The book reports on the results of the PIR/Green (modified OECD) model showing how equity benefited efficiency in the context of the carbon market. In January 1997 I publish a *Financial Times* article, 'The Greening of the Bretton Woods' where I attribute the origins of the global warming problem to the global trade in resources following the creation of the Bretton Woods institutions. Here once again I propose the creation of the carbon market.

The *Financial Times* article creates a larger impact than I could have fathomed. It attracts the interest and support of Mohamed El Ashry, then the Director of the Global Environmental Facility of the World Bank. The fall-out from this article leads me to organize, along with Columbia's Earth Institute, a small but important meeting at the Rockefeller Foundation's Bellagio Conference house on a beautiful Italian lake. The meeting includes the movers and shakers of the time, such as Tom Lovejoy who today leads the Heinz Foundation and Hazel Henderson, a brilliant economist, futurist and creator of *Ethical Markets Media* television series. The purpose of the meeting is to execute the plan in my article for creating a carbon market, and an International Bank of Environmental Settlements, to support its banking aspects, such as the borrowing and lending of carbon rights. In mid 1997 I become a lead author of the IPCC and attend several meetings for their next Assessment Report.

During 1997 I also work with Exxon representatives trying fruitlessly to change their views about whether the global warming threat is real. The same year The Earth Institute hires a publicist named David Fenton, who later goes on to create the famous moveon.org political website. At the end of the year, it sends a delegation to Kyoto for the December 1997 COP meetings.

Kyoto is grey and the weather is somewhat sticky. There are hundreds of earnest non-governmental organization (NGO) participants at the COP meeting, in the streets near them, and all over this beautiful city. I am part of The Earth Institute's delegation, together with Peter Eisenberger and Rick Fairbanks, both famous physicists. Eisenberger is at the time Vice Provost at Columbia University, Founding Director of the Earth Institute and Director of the Lamont Doherty Earth Observatory at Columbia University.

In Kyoto I continue with an unending stream of presentations, press conferences and interviews to the global press on my carbon market concept, which is attracting a lot of attention. These interviews are published in a number of newspapers worldwide and appear on several radio and TV shows. I give a 'side event' presentation at the COP that is very well attended. It all happens under a huge white tent, like a circus, and the floor is covered with wood shavings. There are journalists everywhere and people from all over the world carry signs expressing concerns for the environmental disaster they see coming.

It seems fair to say that people do not really understand much of what I am agitating about, although they are favourably predisposed to give me a hearing. I am basically working alone in this task of trying to create the carbon market of the Kyoto Protocol. Except for my colleagues at The Earth Institute, who are in Kyoto with me, and several of my UNFCCC colleagues such as Raul Estrada Oyuela and Jean-Charles Hourcade, both of whom have worked with me since the OECD 1993 meetings and now have official roles as the lead negotiator and French representative respectively, I do not know many other people, but I am familiar on a first name basis with many of the official negotiators of the developing nations. I talk to all the UN representatives at every occasion I can, particularly Raul Estrada Oyuela, who is getting more and more worried about the ability to reach an agreement, but is adamant against the carbon market approach, and Jean-Charles Hourcade, who is rather young and willing to hear my carbon market enthusiasm, apparently on the strength of my work in international trade and social choice, which he professed to admire. I have lunch with Amory Lovins and with other well-known figures from the energy industry. My colleague William Nordhaus from Yale University is also there, as is James Cameron, a British attorney who represented the group of island nations of the world in the UNFCCC Kyoto Process. Also present is Ambassador Dasgupta, who represents India in the negotiations, the IPCC Chairman Robert Watson, who later becomes Senior Scientific Advisor on the Environment to the World Bank, Urs Luterbacher, a reputed political scientist from Geneva, Jacques Weber, an excellent French economist and Kilaparti Ramakrishna, an environmental attorney who advises Ambassador Raul Estrada Oyuela and goes on to become a Senior Advisor to the Environmental Law and Conventions at the United Nations Environment Programme in Nairobi.

At the end there is a crisis: the feared deadlock between the industrial and the developing nations, the North and the South. The same problem exists today and is the cause of the impasse between the US and China. I am acting as an unofficial adviser to the UNFCCC COP in Kyoto and I am also well recognized in my role as a lead author of the IPCC. In this role I gather psychological strength and address Raul Estrada Oyuela head on. He is friendly and willing to hear me. I tell him why the carbon market approach is like a two-sided coin and the only possible solution to the dilemma he faces, because it could be supported by both the industrial and the developing nations. He listens with interest and sympathy but is emotionally set against it. I insist that it is the only solution and explain to him that I had agitated enough with the developing nations (known as the Group of 77, or G77) negotiators to know that they would support it and had also discussed with the US Senate and Congress, the US Treasury and the Department of State to know that it would fly in the US as well. Raul listens. I explain that the only remaining thorn is Europe. That is where I have done less work and Europeans are more adamant against markets, which they view as a new-fangled US excuse or trick to avoid abiding by carbon emission limits. His response is 'we will see'. To his credit, Raul considers any position and evaluates it fairly.

As the meetings progress, it becomes clear that the negotiators are deadlocked. The industrial nations do not want limits on their emissions since most of the energy they use is fossil fuel-based and they have no intention to sacrifice economic growth. But developing nations are even more adamantly opposed to accepting an emissions limit, which they see as historically unfair and a way to condemn their people to poverty and the trap of underdevelopment.

Result!

On 10 December, the last day of the conference, the general mood is sombre. Along with many others who understand the seriousness of the situation, I stand quite late at night, in the area just outside the large negotiation room, expecting to hear of a breakthrough that does not happen. It is truly sobering. Then at about 10 p.m. Jean-Charles Hourcade comes out of the negotiating room, which has graded seating like a theatre, and invites me in.

Professor Hourcade is a well known and highly regarded economist and French government official. He is an intelligent and original thinker. Since the 1993 OECD meeting Jean-Charles has known about my proposal for the carbon market and the innovation that this entails, in the sense of trading a global public good, namely the carbon concentration in the planet's atmosphere. He knows about the attendant issue of equity and efficiency involving the industrial and developing nations; he accepts the consistency of this issue with Article 4 of the 1992 Climate Convention, which gives the developing nations a preferential role.

Jean-Charles asks me to write a description of the carbon market to include in the draft of the Kyoto Protocol. He is one of three members of the contact group between the EU and US and needs me to prepare wording that will help the Europeans agree with the market approach, and that can provide the flexibility that the US requires before accepting emissions limits. It is truly the eleventh hour of the Kyoto negotiations, because the meetings are ending the very next day. The agreement is difficult to achieve, particularly with the US, and the introduction of the carbon market is invaluable in reaching it. This is where my work of several years proposing the carbon market, at the UN and the OECD, making presentations to the US Congress and Senate, proposing the carbon market structure to the US Treasury and Department of State, actually pays off.

I sit down on the steps of the negotiating room, and begin to write. My words become the basis of Article 17 in the Kyoto Protocol, which describes emissions trading and how the COP will develop the carbon marketing mechanism. The introduction of the carbon market saves the day. It creates a measure of flexibility that leads the US to sign the Protocol. The US feels it can trade its way through the problem: if it cannot meet the limits, it can buy rights to emit from other nations. As the developing nations have no limits on emissions they have preferential treatment, so they sign as well. According to Hourcade, my role was critical to convincing the US and European representatives, who then also sign on to the Kyoto Protocol. The introduction of the CDM provides the added flexibility to integrate developing nations into the carbon market framework, so they can benefit from technology transfers from industrial nations without facing emissions limits.[9] The 160 nations' representatives in Kyoto thus reach a historic agreement.

On 11 December 1997 The Kyoto Protocol is born, voted for by 160 nations. Industrialized countries agree to cut their emissions of six key greenhouse gases by an average of 5.2 per cent. Under the terms of the agreement each country, except for developing countries, committed to reducing emissions by a certain percentage below their 1990 emissions levels by the period 2008–2012. Notably, the US Congress at the time voted 95 to 0 against any treaty that didn't commit developing countries to 'meaningful' cuts in emissions.

In terms of the EU and the US, the Kyoto Protocol adopts the targets proposed by the EU, but the overall structure comes from the US. Indeed the overall structure follows my market strategy and in this sense it follows the US market position, modified by a more favourable treatment of the developing nations in terms of no emission limits and the addition of the CDM. The CDM allows industrial nations to receive credits for proven emission reduction projects that are carried out in developing nations. These credits can be traded in the emissions market, so they carry all the advantages of the trading system without emission limits on developing nations.

The protocol has a flexible and market-oriented architecture. The structure of the Kyoto Protocol is an agreement on emission limits country-by-country, a great achievement for its lead negotiator, Raul Estrada Oyuela, with three flexibility mechanisms to accommodate those nations that on a given year may be above their limits, while maintaining fixed global limits: (i) joint implementation, (ii) the carbon market and (iii) the CDM. The most important and innovative feature of the Kyoto Protocol feature is the carbon market which, together with the CDM, achieves the level of equity that is needed to achieve market efficiency in using the planet's atmosphere.

The developing nations do not trade in the carbon market because they have no limits on emissions themselves. Only the OECD nations do. Yet the developing nations participate in the carbon market through the Clean Development Mechanism (CDM) that allows businesses in rich countries to offset their emissions by funding clean energy projects in developing nations. In the Kyoto Protocol, the CDM is the only link between the industrial and the developing nations. It is the best hope for the future. It creates incentives for developing nations to adopt clean technologies and 'leapfrog' into the future, using a cleaner form of development than the industrial nations used to develop themselves.

Ambassador Raul Estrada Oyuela achieves his mandate of reaching an agreement in Kyoto acting against his own convictions. He does so – as a true professional diplomat – using the carbon market as the two-sided coin that resolves the conflict between the North and the South, and against his own anti-carbon market opinion. The carbon market helps him reach the agreement and the Kyoto Protocol is born.

Post Kyoto

In 2001 the newly elected US President George W. Bush renounces the Kyoto Protocol stating that it will damage the US economy. To date the US has not ratified the Protocol. That same year the third IPCC Assessment Report declares that the evidence that global warming over the previous 50 years has been fuelled by human activities is stronger than ever.

The Kyoto Rules are finalized in 2001 at COP 7 in Marrakech. The Marrakech Accords provide no quantitative limits on emissions trading, significant credits (removal units) for forest and cropland management, caps on CDM or credits for sink activities and no credits for avoided deforestation. The current situation is of growing scientific concern; the evidence continues to reinforce the genuine threat of global warming: only a handful of outliers now dispute these findings. Although Kyoto has now entered into force, without the US and without limits on developing nations, the Protocol will not be sufficient to prevent climate change.

In 2003 Europe experiences one of the hottest summers on record that causes widespread drought and heat waves. As a direct result 30,000 people die.

In 2005, following ratification by Russia in November 2004, the Kyoto Protocol becomes a legally binding treaty. America and Australia continue their refusal to sign up, claiming that reducing emissions would damage their economies.

By 2007 175 countries have ratified the Kyoto Treaty. Under its newly elected Prime Minister Kevin Rudd, who ran a campaign based on changing Australia's policy towards the Kyoto Protocol, Australia too ratifies the treaty. The IPCC Report for a fourth time states that, 'warming of the climate is unequivocal' and that the levels of temperature and sea rise in the 21st century will depend on the extent or limit of emissions in the coming years. Former Vice President Al Gore and the IPCC jointly win the Nobel Peace Prize for services to the global environment.

At an earlier Convention of the Parties in Buenos Aires, the US was completely unwilling to discuss the post 2012 period. And it was joined in this position by important developing nations such as India. Yet in Bali in December 2007, the Convention of the Parties of the UNFCCC decides on a so-called Bali roadmap, to arrive at the terms for a post 2012 agreement by the end of 2009. A great step forward is achieved when the largest emitter in the world, the US, agrees to join this effort by the 2009 target. This is the first sign of US cooperation with the Kyoto Process since the US signed the Protocol in Kyoto on 11 December 1997. There are currently over 40 proposals for future climate change efforts.

In **2008** Australia becomes the first nation to create its own internal carbon market to start trading in 2010. Meanwhile, 414sq km (160 sq mi) of the Wilkins Shelf breaks away from the Antarctic coast. Scientists are concerned that climate change may be happening faster than previously thought.

Following the Bali roadmap, negotiators from 180 countries launch formal negotiations towards a new treaty to mitigate climate change at the Bangkok Climate Change Talks in April 2008. At this meeting the European Union announces their desire to cap or otherwise reduce the CDM transfers to developing nations, which amounted to about $9 billion until 2007 and to $18 billion in 2007, arguing that Europe needs to spur new technologies because simply paying for offsets elsewhere won't solve the problem. Yet business interests are now working to preserve and expand the CDM programme as the EU proposals move through the European Parliament. At the time of writing, Ambassador Raul Estrada Oyuela is still opposed to the concept of the carbon market as part of the global climate negotiations.

Important Milestones in International Climate Negotiations

1988: Intergovernmental Panel on Climate Change (IPCC) establishes the scientific basis of climate negotiations.

1992: United Nations Framework Convention on Climate Change (UNFCCC) is established.

1995: Conference of the Parties to the Convention (COP) 1 in Berlin establishes the goal of reaching a climate agreement agreement by 1997.

1995: First definitive statement that climate change is caused by human action.

1997: COP 3 in Kyoto – Kyoto Protocol is born.

2001: The Marrakech Conference establishes the Kyoto rules.

2005: The Kyoto Protocol becomes international law.

2007: The Bali roadmap is established for reaching a post-Kyoto agreement by 2009.

2012: End of the Kyoto Protocol Provisions – future to be decided.

Behind the institutional façade, the parties of the climate negotiations followed predictable patterns of behaviour, most of which continue to this date. It is useful to understand these patterns because they explain where we are today, how we got here and what can and should be done for the future of the climate negotiations. As already mentioned, the future of the climate negotiations is as uncertain as the climate evolution. Perhaps even more pressing is that at present the Kyoto Protocol's provisions expire in 2012 and there is a big question mark over the future.

We can, and must, expand on Kyoto's initial provisions. But to forge global agreement, we must first identify how to reconcile the needs of developed and developing countries. Kyoto's innovative carbon market, a source of confusion, consternation and also an important measure of success, provides the mechanism to achieve this. The carbon market is a path forward.

The next chapters will explain the economic changes unleashed by the carbon market and the risks that Kyoto faces today.

Kyoto and its Carbon Market

4

The Kyoto Protocol has the potential to change the way we use energy and resolve global warming. It breaks new ground. It is the first international agreement based on the creation of a new global market, a market for trading rights to use the planet's atmosphere.

The carbon market became international law in 2005 and seems ready to become the largest commodity market in the world. According to Bart Chilton, commissioner of the US Commodities Futures Trading Commission, 'even with conservative assumptions, this could be a $2 trillion futures market in relatively short order.'[1]

The carbon market has some unique properties. It is a market based on the trade of a *global public good* – global carbon concentration reduction. The properties that distinguish global public goods from all other private goods that are commonly traded, such as grain, houses, machines and stocks, for example, have important implications for market behaviour. In a market for global public goods, equity and efficiency are inextricably tied in ways that can unite the interests of rich and poor, businesses and environmentalists.[2]

Carbon markets are controversial institutions. Many businesses fear them but in reality they are quite simple. Each trader has emissions limits; those who over-emit have to buy rights from those who under-emit. This penalizes the bad guys and compensates the good guys with minimal government intervention. In a nutshell, the idea is to use Adam Smith's famous invisible hand,[3] the hand of the market. This invisible hand can join the interests of the business sector with the social interests of environmentalists like nothing has done thus far. A similar but different system has worked successfully at the Chicago Board of Trade since 1993. Its sulphur dioxide market decreased acid rain in the US in a very cost-effective way, using a simple cap-and-trade system that is quite different from the carbon market as explained below.

Yes, make no mistake. The carbon market is all about Adam Smith's green hand. But the green hand needs a bit of help to do its magic. The market could not function without binding emission limits on the traders.

The purpose of caps on industrial nations' emissions is to guarantee that global emissions will not exceed levels that could risk catastrophic climate change. Industrial nations emit the large majority of carbon emissions in the world today, and the Protocol provides caps for all industrial nations. This is the feature of the carbon market that environmentalists favour. Of course the Kyoto cap requires that the nations that signed the Protocol in 1997, which include the US, ratify the Protocol and obey the emissions limits accordingly. Almost all industrial nations have ratified it, including Australia, which held out until 2007. The glaring exception is the US, which has not ratified Kyoto yet, but nevertheless agreed at the UN meetings in Bali in December 2007 to join the Kyoto Process and arrive at a solution by the end of 2009. Barack Obama's new administration has announced his intention to make this matter a priority and to use the cap-and-trade system. The US is the largest emitter in the world and therefore its ratification of the Kyoto Protocol will have a measurable impact on global emissions.

But for many business leaders carbon markets are a source of fear and loathing. The fears are about sharply increased costs of doing business, especially for electricity and commodity producers, which are central to the economy but generate substantial carbon emissions. They will have to pay for their emissions. There are also concerns about the volatility of carbon prices when the market starts trading in their own nations. Carbon prices would increase commodity prices and business costs. The concerns of private industry are real and must be addressed.

At the same time, climate change is a real concern as is the continued extraction of resources from the world's fragile ecosystems. Some business leaders perceive potential gains in technological innovation and profitable opportunities arising from the carbon market. They are right. The largest investors in the world are betting a substantial percentage of their risk capital in the renewable energy sector, a sector that has increased in importance from 4 per cent to 18 per cent of total Silicon Valley investments in just four years. Clean energy is arguably the fastest growing area of business in the world today. According to the UNEP, the level of investment is on track to be as high as $450 billion per year by 2012 and $600 billion per year by 2020, replacing existing infrastructure valued at $43 trillion.[4]

How can business opinion sustain such a polarized view of the situation? Is the carbon market a villain or a hero? Both views are right. Each looks at the carbon market with a different lens: the 'before' lens and the 'after' lens. Before the carbon market, the uncertainty can be damaging to business. There are risks and perceived costs and no benefits. Yet as the carbon market starts to operate, it creates a price signal. A price signal means a market price that signals through its level (high or low) the real costs, the real scarcity or the real value of a commodity or whatever is traded. For example, before the carbon market was created, there was no market price to signal the real costs of emitting carbon. There was no signal about this cost because there was no market price for carbon. Once the carbon market was introduced and it started trading in the European Union Trading System (EUTS), a market price emerged (about $30 per ton of carbon emitted) and the cost of carbon was 'signalled' through the carbon price to the entire economy. This carbon price ($30) signals how costly it is to the economy to emit carbon and how costly it is to remove carbon once it is emitted into the atmosphere. The price signal makes cleaner technologies more profitable than the rest. Clean technologies do not pay for emissions. Emitters do. And therefore, when the carbon market operates, Adam Smith's green hand rewards under-emitters and penalizes over-emitters, aligning business and environmental interests. Not a small feat.

The opportunities are open to all, and the rewards can be very substantive once the transition from the 'before' to the 'after' is completed. The IEA predicts that an energy revolution arising from worldwide restructuring of the power plant sector, a $43 trillion infrastructure, will become a major business opportunity. Using the economic incentives created by the carbon market to make a profit while doing good would give a major boost to businesses. Business can react very positively to such a market-based scheme.

But for this to happen we need to extend the Kyoto Protocol beyond 2012, because regional carbon markets, such as the EU carbon market and the national Australian carbon market, cannot achieve much without the global carbon market of the Kyoto Protocol. Why? Because unless there is a global agreement on emissions limits, there is little reason for a single nation to limit its emissions, as no nation can resolve global warming on its own. And therefore there is little reason for any nation to have a national carbon market on its own. In addition, national carbon prices will always match global carbon prices, so no national market can set prices on its own. All carbon markets will derive from the Kyoto Protocol global carbon market, and none will exist as efficiently without it. It is as simple as that.

The global carbon market began when the Kyoto Protocol came into force in 2005 and in the EUTS has traded over $80 billion so far. It is the crucial component of the Kyoto Protocol that sets it apart from all other international agreements. And it is the force compelling Australia, the UK and soon possibly the USA to introduce their own national carbon markets.

How Kyoto's Carbon Market Works

Because of its historic importance, the negotiation of the Protocol naturally involved drama, suspense and intrigue. However, as Raul

Estrada Oyuela reminds us, the Kyoto Protocol is the product of 30 months of complex negotiations and of a climactic last minute adoption.[5] Its articles and paragraphs, therefore, need careful interpretation and further elaboration.

Step One: Limiting Emissions, Nation-by-Nation

The Kyoto Protocol is based on the principle that international cooperation is needed to combat climate change. This was set forth by the 1992 United Nations Framework Convention on Climate Change (UNFCCC), which explained the objective of the Kyoto Protocol, as follows:

> The ultimate objective of this Convention and any related legal instruments that the Conference of the Parties may adopt is to achieve … stabilization of greenhouse gas concentrations in the atmosphere at a level that would prevent dangerous anthropogenic interference with the climate system. Such a level should be achieved within a time-frame sufficient to allow ecosystems to adapt naturally to climate change, to ensure that food production is not threatened and to enable economic development to proceed in a sustainable manner.[6]

The first step for negotiators of the Kyoto Protocol was therefore to establish quantified emissions reduction commitments from participating nations. The total level had to be enough to reduce the threat of catastrophic climate change. Countries had agreed to voluntary emission reductions back at the 1992 Earth Summit but most nations failed to meet their voluntary targets, and emissions in most countries actually increased.[7]

By the time the Kyoto Protocol was negotiated in 1997, it was very clear that voluntary targets did not suffice and binding limits were necessary.

Without a global cap on emissions, there could be no carbon market. The carbon market trades 'rights' to emit carbon into the

Annex 1 Emissions Target*

Country	Target (in per cent)
EU-15**, Bulgaria, Czech Republic, Estonia, Latvia, Liechtenstein, Lithuania, Monaco, Romania, Slovakia, Slovenia, Switzerland	-8
United States***	-7
Canada, Hungary, Japan, Poland	-6
Croatia	-5
New Zealand, Russian Federation, Ukraine	0
Norway	+1
Australia	+8
Iceland	+10

* Target is defined as percentage change from 1990 emissions level during the commitment period, 2008-2012.
** The 15 member states of the EU have reached their own agreement about how to distribute the 8 per cent emissions target amongst themselves.
*** The US has announced its intention to not ratify the Kyoto Protocol.

atmosphere. These rights establish who has the right to emit what. Trading cannot begin until there is a clear agreement on the number of tonnes of carbon dioxide that each nation has the right to produce. Each seller must be able to demonstrate it has 'title' to the carbon emissions rights it sells. This means that every nation must have a well determined limit, otherwise it could sell infinite amounts and no market would exist.

Article 3 of the Kyoto Protocol specifies the amount of carbon that each country can emit. These are written as a required percentage reduction from 1990 emission levels (see 'Annex 1 Emissions Target' table on p82) for Annex I countries. These are mostly the industrialized countries and countries with economies in transition. They had to reduce emissions by an average 5.2 per cent of 1990 levels during the period 2008–2012.

Some nations, such as Australia, could increase their emissions from 1990 levels.

At first glance a reduction of 5.2 per cent sounds like a very modest target. But compared with the 24 per cent increase in global emissions that was the 'business as usual' scenario over the period, the real reduction required by the Kyoto Protocol is actually closer to 30 per cent.[8]

The Kyoto Protocol counts net emissions. Each nation gets credit for carbon removals by natural sinks (sinks are reservoirs of carbon that reduce atmospheric concentration of carbon, such as oceans and forests) – from land use activities and forestry. It states:

> Net changes in greenhouse gas emissions ... resulting from direct human-induced land-use change and forestry activities, limited to afforestation, reforestation and deforestation since 1990 ... shall be used to meet the commitments under this Article of each Party included in Annex I.[9]

This provided a degree of flexibility in reducing emissions, and much needed incentives to adopt sustainable land-use practices and conservation of forests. Annex I countries are effectively penalized if they deforest, since emissions from deforestation will count against their Kyoto emissions targets.[10]

As negotiators soon realized, it is difficult to establish a global emissions cap that is both fair and capable of preventing climate change. Global emissions caps were not easy to achieve. They had to meet scientific targets and protect poor nations. The Kyoto Protocol had to include policies and measures in such a way to minimize 'adverse effects' on climate change and trade, as well as social, environmental and economic 'impacts' on other parties, especially developing nations.[11]

The carbon concentration in the planet's atmosphere has a distinguishing and unusual feature: it is the same the world over. In other words, there is no way that one nation could choose one carbon concentration and another nation choose a different one.

Whether they like it or not, all nations are exposed to the same carbon concentration in the atmosphere. It doesn't matter how much emission a nation produces or what they can afford. The atmosphere does not distinguish between emissions produced, or emissions reduced, in the US, China, Bolivia or Australia. Each nation emits a different amount, this is true, but the ultimate carbon concentration that we are exposed to is the same for everyone on the planet. The laws of physics – nature's laws – reign supreme and trump the geopolitical and economic realities of energy use.

This unusual feature makes the carbon market unique and makes it a market for a global public good. The quality of the atmosphere is the ultimate equalizer and unifier; it is one and the same for everyone on the planet.[12]

In setting a global emissions cap poor nations are forced to accept a lower level of global emissions than they can afford. From this unusual feature it follows that developing nations must be treated more favourably than industrial nations in terms of what they emit.[13] Otherwise they will not agree, and unless we all agree, the world will never reach the lower level that we need in order to prevent carbon change. This is why developing nations must have preferential rights to emit. Forcing developing nations to emit less proves to be inefficient for the entire world as well as unfair, unless offsetting measures are implemented. This feature also makes the carbon market unlike any other market we ever saw before; it is a market where efficiency and fairness are tied to each other.

Carbon Markets or Carbon Taxes?

Why did the Kyoto Protocol embrace the market approach to emissions reduction? The Protocol could have simply assigned emissions rights nation-by-nation to cap global emissions at acceptable levels. It could have stopped there, without creating an institution in which those rights could be traded. Indeed, the debates in Kyoto were heading in that direction until the American negotiators insisted that there would be no agreement without emissions trading. The US demanded additional flexibility and this is what the market provided.

Think of it this way: the world needs to impose limit emissions no matter what. Each nation has to agree to limit its emissions; this is a must. Otherwise we cannot make a dent in global warming.

But once emissions limits are established nation-by-nation the market approach becomes a very natural add-on. It has little cost and great benefits. Trading the right to emit allows a flexibility that is not available otherwise. A nation could one year be above its limit and the next below it – it is difficult to predict. With the market approach, as the total of all nations' emissions is below the global limit, each nation can fluctuate in its emissions – up one year and down the next. This becomes a very natural and desirable flexibility. It certainly fits very well the interests of the US, the largest emitter in the world, for whom flexibility becomes very valuable. This simple rationale won the day.

The foundations for the carbon market began with the assignment of binding emission limits to participating countries. This established a firm cap on global emissions – something that most environmentalists favoured. The cap is the only way to avoid the risks of catastrophic climate change. This alone makes the market approach more attractive than carbon taxes, since taxes cannot guarantee aggregate emission levels.[14]

This is a well-known and universal truth. Indeed, one of the main differences between the cap-and-trade approach and emission taxes is the degree of assurance they offer about world pollution levels. With a cap-and-trade system the aggregate level of pollution is fixed by the total number of emission rights issued. If global emission rights are capped at six billion tonnes of carbon dioxide, and if the system is enforced, total global emissions will not exceed six billion tonnes. That is all. The international community will always know how much emission reduction will be achieved in advance. The total amount of global carbon emissions is predictable. But there is also an important aspect of the market approach that cannot be known in advance: the cost to emitters of reducing their emissions to the specified level. This cost is captured by the price of the emissions permit. This price will be determined by the forces of supply and demand. In general, it cannot be predicted in advance with any accuracy.

Contrast this to the situation with a carbon tax. The cost to the polluter is given by the tax and is known with certainty. But the aggregate amount of pollution cannot be predicted. As long as the cost of reducing a tonne of carbon is less than the tax an emitter has to pay to emit that tonne, the emitter will reduce emissions. Since we don't know in advance what the cost of reducing emissions will be, we have no way of predicting how emitters will respond to the pollution tax and by how much they will reduce their emissions. This is a key difference between a cap-and-trade approach and a pollution tax.

Here is a simple example: consider a tax on cigarettes. A cigarette tax does not guarantee a reduction in smoking, it just provides a disincentive to purchase cigarettes. In theory, if we raise the cost of smoking people will reduce their consumption of cigarettes. This is the hope. But if we fail to set the price high enough, or if people choose to smoke despite the penalty, the consumption of cigarettes will not decrease. It could even increase. It is a similar story with income tax and with estate taxes. We cannot predict that people will work less, or leave less inheritance because of these taxes – and even if they did, we cannot predict by how much.

The same is true with carbon taxes. Carbon taxes will penalize emissions producers and provide incentives to reduce emissions, with the aim that carbon emissions will subside. But carbon taxes give us no guarantee in advance that global emissions will decrease as much as we need them to do in order to avoid the risk of climate catastrophe. Given the urgency of the climate crisis and what is at stake, we don't have the time or leeway for error to keep adjusting the carbon tax until we settle on the tax rate per tonne of carbon that induces our desired emissions reduction. This could take 30 years. Regarding climate change, one thing we know with reasonable confidence is how much global emissions must decrease by to minimize the most serious risks of climate change. It makes sense to start with what we know and build our strategy around it. This is what the carbon market allows us to do.

In situations of great political sensitivity, knowing the cost of policy intervention to industry and commerce may be essential: this is an argument for pollution taxes. In situations of great sensitivity of the environment to pollution, knowing the aggregate level of pollution that will result from a policy may be essential: this is an argument for emissions trading. The latter point is crucial to understanding why the carbon market, rather than the carbon tax, is more appropriate for addressing climate change. There are critical thresholds in the planet's climate system. If we pass these thresholds the consequences are irreversible. We need the assurance of a fixed global emissions cap to minimize the risks that we will surpass these critical thresholds.[15]

Another powerful political sensitivity surrounds the creation of a global taxing authority, which would be necessary should the carbon taxes approach be followed. This seems almost impossible to visualize, let alone achieve. It could be as difficult as the creation of a second United Nations. It is difficult enough for citizens in nations such as the US to accept a global authority on international security issues. A global tax authority would be universally opposed. The concern is the creation of a global bureaucracy that collects funds from all the nations in the world, corresponding to about 1 per cent of the world gross domestic product (GDP) or about $1 trillion, and allocates them appropriately to avert global warming. How likely is it that such a tax bureaucracy will emerge any time soon? Lack of trust in a global governmental entity of this sort could sink the entire effort. By contrast, the carbon market sails easily through these difficulties because by its own nature it needs no bureaucratic intermediaries. The bad guys who over-emit pay the good guys who under-emit, simply and directly. There are no tax authorities in the middle, collecting funds and deciding what to do with them.

More generally, it is the politics and underlying physical realities of climate change that mitigate in favour of a carbon market, rather than a carbon tax. The US finds the market-based approach consistent with its prevailing market-orientated approach to economic policy. Tax-based approaches are an anathema to a political climate in Washington that is strongly predisposed against taxes. Without the inclusion of the carbon market in the Kyoto Protocol, the US would have walked away from the table. In Europe, the tradition is quite different. Carbon taxes are more consistent with the European approach to economic policy. Most European governments historically have had no natural affinity for market-based approaches to pollution management, having perceived markets to be part of the problem rather than part of the solution. Hence, the concept of a cap-and-trade regime was much less familiar in Europe. This, in part, explains the hesitancy European negotiators expressed about Kyoto's carbon market.

Step Two: Allocating Emissions Rights

In establishing a global cap on emissions, the negotiators of the Kyoto Protocol had to decide, at the same time, how to distribute those rights between countries. One would think that the two issues are separate, that finding a global cap is a different issue from deciding who gets to emit what. Surprisingly, however, this is not so. It turns out that these two issues are actually closely linked physically, economically and politically. These links are quite important for understanding the challenges and the opportunities presented by the global climate negotiations.

Furthermore, in practice, the two issues were closely linked in the negotiation of the Kyoto Protocol and these links permitted the Protocol to be successfully negotiated in the first place. In December 1997, global caps were negotiated at the same time as the acceptance of each nation cap, nation-by-nation. This happened for a very good reason. The two are neatly tied up together. It is extremely important for reasons of equity to provide preferential treatment to developing nations. Otherwise they would not have agreed to the lower emissions that the Kyoto Protocol was all about. Developing nations feel it is a matter of historical fairness that they should not be asked to clean up after the carbon emissions that industrial nations produced during their own period of industrialization. Both historically and currently, industrialized nations, which house only 20 per cent of the world population, emit the majority of the world emissions because they consume the majority of the world's energy. The inequity in the world's use of resources is already a source of friction. Asking the developing nations to clean after the industrial nations would only add to the conflict. There is an additional practical argument. Even if developing nations were to stop all their carbon this would still not make a dent in the global warming problem because developing nations emit so little. In fact, all Africa's citizens together emit 3 per cent of the world emissions and a similar amount is emitted by Latin America's.[16]

For many people, this information may induce cognitive dissonance. The first major problem that comes to the minds of most people on the issue of global warming is increasing carbon emissions. Two popular myths still prevail on the subject of carbon emissions:

1) Poor countries have higher populations and therefore, consume most of the world's energy.
2) Similarly, GDP per capita and carbon emissions are unrelated.

However natural they may seem to be, these two arguments are completely untrue. To address the first issue, according to the IEA, as of 2003, developing nations only consumed 41 per cent of the world's energy. This might seem high, but keep in mind that the developing world contains roughly 80 per cent of the world's population. The industrial nations with less than 20 per cent of the world's population use 60 per cent of the world's energy.

Rich nations are responsible for the majority of the world's carbon dioxide emissions. The over-consumption of natural resources manifests itself in other areas as well. According to the World Resource Institute (WRI), which gathers its data from the UN

Food and Agricultural Organization (FAO), as of 2002, rich nations consume 43 per cent of the world's meat.[17] And meat production causes 18 per cent of the world's carbon emissions, more than the entire transportation sector of the world economy including all cars, ships, aeroplanes and trucks.[18]

Emission rights are highly valuable commodities, especially when those rights can be traded in a global carbon market. The allocation of emissions rights is a potent tool for redistributing wealth between nations. The more emissions rights we give a country, the more income it can earn by selling this valuable commodity in international markets. As we'll see in Chapter 5, we can harness this potential of Kyoto to close the global income divide between the poor and rich nations.

Who Should Reduce Carbon Emissions: The Rich or The Poor?

Whereas the size of the global emissions cap should, at least theoretically, be based on climate science, the issue of how to distribute the emissions rights has an interesting feature: it can be used to ensure efficient market solutions.

This provides an objective answer to a seemingly subjective question about how to divide emissions rights between countries. The division of rights is associated with the total amount of rights for the world as a whole. In the early part of the 20th century the great Swedish economist Eric Lindahl explained why efficiency dictates that lower income people should have more rights to use public goods. The French economist Pigou explained this issue as well in the context of taxes. In 1992, Chichilnisky, Heal and Starrett came to a similar conclusion about carbon markets.[19] In simple words, when dealing with public goods, equity is connected with efficiency. Perhaps not coincidentally, the negotiators of the Kyoto Protocol came to exactly the same conclusion in December 1997.

Negotiators could have adopted several different approaches to allocating emissions rights. For example, one approach would be to establish caps based on equal percentage reductions for all nations. In which case, a country like Bangladesh, where the average citizen makes $1,400 per year, would have to reduce its emissions by the same percentage as a country like Germany, where per capita income is $34,400. Given the vast income disparities that persist worldwide, this approach is considered highly unfair by most.

Others have proposed allocating emissions caps on the basis of population size. In this case, China, with a population of 1.3 billion, would be given many more rights to use the atmosphere than the US, with a population of 300 million. In fact they would be given four times as many rights under this scheme. Many have argued that this is fair, but it may not be politically feasible. It is hard to imagine the rich nations of the world ceding that much advantage to the more populous developing nations. The right to emit carbon is the right to use fossil fuel energy, such as coal, of which China has some of the largest deposits in the world.

In practice, how did negotiators establish emissions caps and allocate emissions rights between countries in the crucial days leading to the 11 December 1997 Kyoto Agreement? Once again, negotiators were guided by the principles of cooperation established by the UNFCCC, which happen to agree with Lindhal and Pigou, as well as with the work of Chichilnisky, Heal and Starett.[20]

The UNFCCC established the principle of 'common but differentiated responsibilities', which recognized that nations have contributed unequally to the build-up of atmospheric greenhouse gas concentrations in the past, and that nations have different abilities to pay for emissions reduction in the present. This principle is the source of the tension between rich and poor countries over whether and how to cap developing country emissions beyond Kyoto's expiration in 2012. Article 3 of the UNFCCC states:

The Parties should protect the climate system for the benefit of present and future generations of humankind, on the basis of equity and in accordance with their common but differentiated responsibilities and respective capabilities. Accordingly, the developed country Parties should take the lead in combating climate change and the adverse effects thereof.

Article 4 of the 1992 Convention establishes that developing nations will not be required to reduce their carbon emissions unless they are compensated for it.

Accordingly, the Kyoto Protocol did not assign mandatory emissions limits to developing nations. This was in recognition of their limited energy use historically and in the present, and their special needs and limitations. It assigned emissions limits to industrialized countries, the 39 Annex I countries that together account for two-thirds of global emissions. Within the group of industrialized nations, individual country commitments vary; but on average countries are required to reduce emissions by 5.2 per cent of 1990 levels during the first commitment period, which runs from 2008 to 2012.

The Kyoto Protocol instructed the industrialized nations to lead the global effort to combat climate change. It demanded that they go first, blaze the path, and share their acquired knowledge and technologies with developing nations so that they too can follow in the near future. But let us remember that the Kyoto Protocol is the product of international negotiation. The different roles it assigns to developed and developing nations reflect the will of the international community. Kyoto is truly remarkable. Not only did it cap global greenhouse gas emissions for the first time in history but it also convinced nations to lay aside differences and embrace a strategy that distributed the burden of emissions reduction fairly but unequally for practical reasons. It made concessions to equity that are almost unprecedented in international affairs. These trailblazing results set precedents that could change the world economy in the 21st century.

Step Three: Flexibility and Efficiency

To design an international climate agreement that enough countries worldwide could support, the negotiators had to solve two issues simultaneously: i) reduce global emissions to avert climate change and distribute them fairly and ii) achieve the greatest degree of flexibility and secure efficiency to achieve the targets at the lowest possible cost. The carbon market solved both issues at once.

Just how does the carbon market guarantee flexibility and efficiency? Even though is it distinct from all other markets, the carbon market is still a market. By their own nature, markets can be efficient mechanisms. This is why markets are the most powerful institutions in the world economy today.

The carbon market has the potential to allocate resources efficiently in the economy. By placing a price on carbon emissions, the carbon market forces us to come to grips with an underlying scarcity we previously had ignored, the atmosphere's finite capacity to absorb our greenhouse gases. It makes us confront the real costs of using fossil fuels, costs that include the damage we inflict on ourselves and on future generations.

It may seem distasteful to assign property rights and a price to such a precious resource as the planet's atmosphere but there is no real alternative. The world economy is a market economy; it relies on the price signal to determine the 'best' or 'most efficient' use of scarce resources. Effectively, the price of carbon in the global economy has been zero until now. Markets have never got a price as wrong as they have the price of carbon! As Oscar Wilde famously said 'An economist is someone who knows the price of everything and the value of nothing'.[21]

Since carbon emissions are a by-product of our energy use and energy is the most important input for economic production, the failure to price carbon right throughout history has led to very inefficient use of resources until now. It is the reason we are in the predicament we are today, racing against time to wean ourselves off fossil fuels. Fossil fuels are very costly to humankind; the costs of global warming, if we include human lives lost, species extinction and irreperable damage to ecosystems, are incalculable. Yet our markets so far have been ignorant of these costs. Imagine where we would be today if we had paid for carbon throughout our history? It is difficult to imagine how different our economies and technologies would look now.

The Clean Development Mechanism and Developing Countries

The logic of emission trading is actually quite simple. Suppose that you have two similar countries, Ecoland and Greentopia, and both are required to reduce their emissions. Ecoland could eliminate all the emissions originating within its borders, and Greentopia could do the same to all emissions within its borders. But what if the costs of reducing emissions in Ecoland are lower than the costs of reducing emissions in Greentopia? We know that there are some technologies for reducing emissions that will cost less than others. Technologies that improve energy efficiency, such as solar and wind energy, fluorescent lightbulbs, improvements to the energy efficiency of homes and buildings and fuel-efficient vehicle standards can conserve fossil fuel use at relatively low cost. Sometimes these options are referred to as 'low-hanging fruit'. What if low-hanging fruit still hangs in Ecoland, but Greentopia has already exhausted its low cost abatement options? What if compared with Greentopia, Ecoland has abundant hydroelectric or wind power capacity that it can substitute for coal or natural gas? There are many possible reasons why one country may be able to curb emissions at lower cost than others. In which case why not save money by having more emissions reduction take place in the countries where it costs least?

Emission trading makes it possible to shift some of Greentopia's emission reduction to Ecoland, such that both countries benefit. Either Greentopia can invest directly in emission reduction inside of Ecoland and apply the emissions reduction to the total amount it is required to do under the Kyoto Protocol, or Ecoland can reduce its emissions and sell its unused user rights to the atmosphere to Greentopia. In either case, Greentopia meets its emissions target at a lower total cost, and Ecoland benefits by selling the emission rights it doesn't need because it has either the resources, the technology or the untapped energy efficiency potential to reduce emissions at relatively low cost.

The Kyoto Protocol allows for emissions trading between industrialized countries – those that have binding emission caps. The Kyoto Protocol also created a mechanism known as Joint Implementation (JI). This is a bilateral form of emissions trading between industrial countries (especially the transitioning economy countries in central and eastern Europe) that is project-based, allowing one country to invest directly in emissions reduction activities in another. However because JI is bilateral trading, and it is unsightly to pair up a powerful rich nation with a poor developing nation in bilateral trading since the power relation seems too skewed, it applies only to industrialized countries – those countries with binding emissions limits. Indeed, Article 6 of the Kyoto Protocol states:

> For the purpose of meeting its commitments under Article 3, any Party included in Annex I may transfer to, or acquire from, any other such Party emission reduction units resulting from projects aimed at reducing anthropogenic emissions by sources or enhancing anthropogenic removals by sinks of greenhouse gases in any sector of the economy...

To provide developing countries with incentives to reduce emissions, and to encourage investment and technologies from North to South, as the Kyoto Protocol was required to do, a mechanism for including developing nations in the global carbon market had to be designed.

The Clean Development Mechanism (CDM), often referred to as the 'Kyoto Surprise', provides the crucial link between developed and developing nations in the global carbon market.[22]

The CDM enables an industrialized country to invest in reducing emissions in developing nations and count the emissions reduction towards its own emissions cap. It is very similar to JI, only it is not bilateral trading as it goes through the carbon market, which is a multilateral market. It defines a role for developing countries in the emerging global carbon market, and it allows for the profitable participation by the private sector. As defined by Article 12:

> The purpose of the clean development mechanism shall be to assist Parties not included in Annex I [developing nations] in achieving sustainable development and in contributing to the ultimate objective of the Convention, and to assist Parties included in Annex I in achieving compliance with their quantified emission limitation and reduction commitment...

The idea for the CDM is straightforward enough. Emitters can save money by investing in lower cost emissions reduction options in developing nations. In return, developing countries benefit from the direct investment in their economies and technology transfers.

In practice, there are several ways that emissions reductions can be financed through the CDM. Developed countries may finance project activities in developing countries and use the resulting emissions credits towards their own emissions targets. Emissions producers within developed countries – for example utility companies – may invest directly in CDM project activities in developing countries and use the resulting emissions credits to demonstrate compliance with their own country's emissions restrictions. (In order for a country to meet its Kyoto target, it is going to have to require emissions reductions by emissions producers within its borders). Alternatively, developing countries themselves can invest in their own emissions reduction projects and market the resulting credits through the CDM. Lastly, CDM project activities may be financed by third parties – often NGOs, development agencies or private for-profit entities – and the resulting emissions credits can be sold in the global carbon market. To date there have been CDM projects involving reforestation, hydropower, methane capture, energy efficiency improvements, and fuel-switching. Examples of such CDM projects are detailed in Chapter 6.

The CDM connects global emissions reduction to the broader goal of sustainable development. It creates incentives for developing nations to adopt clean technologies and move into the future on a more ecologically sustainable development path than the one the industrialized nations used during their development. Yet the CDM remains one of the most controversial parts of the Kyoto Protocol. Why?

The main issue is that so far the majority of the CDM projects, approximately 60 per cent, have gone to China.[23] This is because the projects that qualify for CDM credits are those that reduce carbon emissions. Since China is by far the largest emitter of all developing nations (approximately 18 per cent of the world emissions) it has most emissions to reduce. Africa as a whole emits only 3 per cent of the global emissions and therefore, today, there is little in terms of CDM that Africa can capture. It can reduce little in terms of emissions because it emits so little. The same is true in Latin America. As described in Chapters 2 and 5, what is required here is to introduce CDM projects that allow 'negative carbon', namely those projects that can reduce carbon over and above what the region emits as a whole. In that case, Africa could reduce 20 per cent of the world emissions even if it emits only 3 per cent itself. This is the solution, but it requires a modest modification of the CDM to allow for such technologies.

Avoiding the Problem?

A main criticism is that the EU must change its technologies to adapt to cleaner forms of energy but the CDM projects are sheltering the EU from going through this technological change. Another important point is that it is imperative that emission credits resulting from CDM investments represent 'reductions in emissions that are additional to any that would occur in the absence of certified project activity'.[24] During the debates in Kyoto, the terms 'paper tonnes' and 'hot air' were used to indicate the importance of verifying emission reductions in all countries participating in trading – especially developing countries. The Kyoto Protocol itself requires verification of the reductions, by the appropriate CDM Accreditation Committee that resides in Bonn. The reason is simple. The CDM allows industrialized countries to substitute emissions reduction within their borders for emissions reduction in the developing world. If the emissions reduction credit they have purchased in the developing world is not based on honest-to-goodness emissions reduction, global emissions will not decrease. If the emissions reduction credits are not legitimate, for example, if countries are selling emission credits for activities that don't reduce emissions, or for activities that do reduce emissions but would have taken place anyway without another country's investment, then the CDM can actually undermine Kyoto's global emissions cap. As with all things where there is money to be made, the incentives for businesses to exaggerate on their claims of deserving carbon credits are high. This is not an indictment of the logic behind the CDM, rather a cautionary tale about its practice. Effective monitoring is, and will continue to be, essential to the judicious use of the CDM but there is no reason to believe that effective monitoring is not possible.

Finally, it is important to point out that there is a misunderstanding regarding emission limits. While it is true that developing nations do not have emissions limits, they do have so-called emission baselines, which measure the expected trend of the business-as-usual baseline of emissions against what the CDM project predicts the reductions to be. The baselines are then used by the CDM accreditation committee to measure the extent of emissions that would otherwise occur without the project.

There is another issue to consider: the basis of the current concerns in the EU. The Kyoto Protocol was designed to shift the burden of emissions reduction more heavily onto the countries that were most responsible for climate change and that were best able to pay for emissions reduction. Will emissions trading allow industrialized countries to escape the burden of costly emissions reduction and forestall the transition away from fossil fuels? Prior to withdrawing from the Kyoto Protocol, the US had indicated that it would purchase most of its required emissions reduction abroad. So, yes, countries can use emissions trading to avoid investing in emissions reduction at home, but only up to a limit. Fortunately there is an easy solution: because emissions trading makes it easier and less expensive for countries to reduce and meet their emission caps we can lower the caps further in the next round of negotiations. We know further emissions reductions are required beyond Kyoto's expiration in 2012. Carbon emission trading, since it lowers compliance costs, improves the likelihood that countries will agree to lower caps in the future.

Nevertheless, the carbon market and its CDM remain controversial, as is shown in the next chapter. The carbon market is a new type of market the likes of which have never been seen before in the world, and we are learning by doing.[25] It is not surprising that there is much to adjust to; Kyoto is, after all, only a first step and not the end of the road.

Ratification and Implementation

Before the Kyoto Protocol could enter into force and become international law – before the emission limits could become binding – the Kyoto Protocol had to be ratified by a number of nations. This had to include enough industrial nations to account for at least 55 per cent of the emissions of that group. This provision was necessary to ensure that emissions reduction would be sufficient, in total, to make it worthwhile for countries to participate. In practice this provision did not give any individual country the ability to veto the Kyoto Protocol but it did give veto right to the US and Russia together. The Kyoto Protocol could enter into force without Russia or without the US, but not without both.

The US is still holding fort against Kyoto, but Russia changed its position. It took eight years from its creation in 1997 for the Kyoto Protocol to become binding. It took this long for enough Annex I countries to ratify the Kyoto Protocol. The European Union, despite its hesitancy over the inclusion of the carbon market, ratified the Kyoto Protocol only months after its negotiation. The US, one of the early signers of the Kyoto Protocol and the chief impetus behind its carbon market, announced its withdrawal from the Kyoto Protocol in 2001, under the leadership of the newly elected republican President George W. Bush. The US's decision dealt a serious blow to the Protocol. Most economists in the US deemed Kyoto dead. It took a great deal of conviction to believe that Bush and his eight-year presidency of the most powerful nation in the world were not as powerful as an international agreement that could stop climate change.

Kyoto was humble but it was more powerful than George W. Bush. President Bush has now left office while Kyoto is international law and its market is growing by leaps and bounds, trading $80 billion so far and about $50 billion annually.[26] Both US presidential candidates in 2008 indicated their willingness to ratify the Protocol. It is a lesson in contemporary history.

The ratification of Kyoto shifted all attention to Russia, the only other country with sufficient emissions in the base year to qualify the Kyoto Protocol for implementation. Russia was in a unique position. De-industrialization following the collapse of the Soviet Union in 1991 had resulted in a significant emissions reduction. This meant that Russia would have an easier time meeting its Kyoto emissions target than it had anticipated. It also meant that Russia was in a position to sell its unused emission rights to other countries through the carbon market.

Russia ratified the treaty in late 2004. The long-awaited Kyoto Protocol entered into force ninety days later on 16 February 2005. As of early 2009, 181 countries have ratified the Kyoto Protocol, including 37 Annex I countries, representing 64 per cent of the emissions of industrialized countries. Australia ratified Kyoto in 2007. Notably absent, of course, is the world's largest greenhouse gas producer, the US. As of this writing, the US and Kazakhstan are the only two Annex I countries that have not yet ratified the Kyoto Protocol.

The State of the Carbon Market

The global carbon market became international law when the Kyoto Protocol entered into force in 2005. How well has Kyoto's carbon market performed since then? Does its reality match its much heralded potential? A few basic numbers summarize how well the carbon market is performing thus far: by the end of 2006, the first full year of trading, the carbon market had grown in value to an estimated $30 billion, three times greater than the previous year. In 2007 it traded $50 billion.

The global carbon market includes several regional markets, all of which were made possible because of Kyoto's provisions for emissions trading and the CDM. The European Union Emissions Trading Scheme (EU ETS) is the largest market at present. Sales and re-sales of European Union emissions allowances in this market reached $25 billion in 2006. The Chicago Climate Exchange (CCX) and the New South Wales market (NSW), smaller markets for voluntary reductions by corporations and individuals, witnessed record trading values and volumes. They grew strongly to an estimated $100 million[27] but they are not expected to play a defining role in the global market.

The real success story was, and continues to be, the trade in emission credits from project-based activities through the CDM, and to a much lesser extent, JI. These projects grew sharply to a value of about $5 billion in 2006. China continues to dominate the CDM market, accounting for 61 per cent of its value. In 2007 the World Bank reported that CDM projects were $15 billion strong. In total over $23 billion has been transferred to developing nations for clean productive projects that reduce the equivalent of 20 per cent of the EU annual emissions.[28]

Who is buying and selling in the carbon markets? At present the main buyers in the carbon market area:

1) European private buyers interested in EU ETS.
2) Government buyers interested in Kyoto compliance.
3) Japanese companies with voluntary commitments under the Keidanren Voluntary Action Plan (see glossary).

4) US multinationals operating in Japan and Europe and preparing in advance for the Regional Greenhouse Gas Initiative (RGGI) in the northeastern US and the mid Atlantic or the California Assembly Bill 32, which aims to establish a state-wide cap on emissions.

5) Power retailers and large consumers regulated by the NSW market.

6) North American companies with voluntary but legally binding compliance objectives in the CCX.

In 2006, European buyers dominated the CDM and JI markets. They accounted for 86 per cent of the market, an increase from 50 per cent in the year 2005. Japanese purchases were only 7 per cent of the CDM market. The UK led the market with about 50 per cent of project-based volumes, followed by Italy with 10 per cent. Private sector buyers, predominantly banks and carbon funds, continued to buy large numbers of CDM assets, while public sector buyers continued to dominate JI purchases.

In addition to financial performance, it is important to evaluate the physical impact of the carbon market in order to keep track of the actual carbon reductions that the market achieved. The CDM market played a main role in this reduction. In contrast to the highly volatile 2006 EU ETS market, project-based credits demonstrated greater price stability, while the volume of transactions grew steadily. But most important is the fact that since 2002, a cumulative 920 million tonnes of carbon, an amount equivalent to 20 per cent of EU emissions in 2004, have been reduced through CDM projects in developing nations at a value of $8 billion.[29] These trends continued and strengthened in 2007, with an additional $15 billion in CDM projects, although once again the majority went to China and very little to Africa or Latin America.

Carbon Prices and Market Stability

Despite the success of the carbon market, carbon prices have fluctuated widely. This is a source of concern for private industry, which seeks firm price signals in order to plan for costs and opportunities. Because the carbon market is so new there is understandably some confusion about how carbon prices are set. Many believe that they are set by free floating supply and demand. While it is true that prices do fluctuate somewhat in the short term with supply and demand forces, it is possible to identify market 'fundamentals' that determine carbon prices.

The key to explaining fluctuations is given by the 2006 behaviour of the carbon markets, where a drop in carbon prices from $30 per tonne to $10 per tonne followed the selection of higher emission caps by the European Union. It is possible to show how carbon markets function to determine carbon prices, and how these prices fluctuate over time.

The main point is that in a fossil-fuel dominated global economy, there are two 'fundamentals' that determine prices in the carbon market: (i) emission caps, which are a measure of scarcity and the extent of demand for 'permits to emit' and (ii) the technology that allows us to transform fossil fuels into goods and services, which gives the 'opportunity cost' of reducing carbon.

Let us consider caps first. The caps are provided by governments, in accordance with their Kyoto Protocol obligations. Governments can decide their own pace for achieving their Kyoto targets and they can establish their own caps accordingly. The lower the caps, the higher the obligation to reduce carbon, and therefore the higher the price of carbon. This is how the market operates. In 2006, the EU discovered that carbon prices were dropping because the caps on carbon emissions were set too high. The EU promised to adjust these caps correspondingly and by lowering emission caps, governments increased the demand for permits and increased the price of carbon.

The second determinant of carbon prices is the technology that transforms energy into goods. This gives the 'opportunity cost' of reducing emissions, namely the goods that we fail to produce because we use less fossil energy, or the cost of carbon capture as discussed in Chapters 2 and 5.

This is how the carbon market works: it provides incentives for the use of clean technologies. It favours technologies that emit less carbon over and above those that emit more. The latter has to pay for its emissions, the former gets rewarded for avoiding emissions.

There is a critical interplay between carbon markets and technology. Technology has an impact on market prices. Reciprocally, the carbon price has an impact on what technology is developed and used. This interplay is at the core of our ability to resolve the global warming issue in the short and the long term, because by using the right technologies we can avert global warming.

What's Next?

Despite its limitations, the Kyoto Protocol has already shown much promise. In its first two years of existence as international law, 2006 and 2007, the carbon market traded $80 billion dollars, representing a 20 per cent reduction of EU annual emissions; it had a transformational effect in technology and reduced emissions and, at the same time, it was able to make a significant wealth transfer of above $23 billion so far towards poor nations for clean and productive projects that reduced global emissions. This transfer is desirable and fair, since the developing nations have emitted small amounts of carbon historically, and currently they use little energy, while they bear a disproportionate burden of the risks of climate change.

All of this was possible because of the magic of the Kyoto Protocol's carbon market. Yet, there is more magic to behold. As we will soon see, Kyoto's carbon market can avert global warming at no net cost to the global economy. It can foster sustainable development and can close the global divide between rich and poor nations. And it can do all this at no cost to the taxpayer, while providing incentives to create and implement the clean technologies of the future.

But attacks on the carbon market and the impasse between China and the US threaten the survival of Kyoto. The suspense in this drama is whether Kyoto will survive its critics – whether it can be saved. Stay tuned.

Kyoto's Uncertain Future

5

Bali is one of the most beautiful places on earth, a large idyllic island in the Indonesian archipelago, home to historic art and mischievous monkeys. But it is also one of the places most vulnerable to rising sea levels from climate change. This was a poignant reminder to climate negotiators of just how much was at stake when they met at the Bali Convention of the Parties (COP) in December 2007. The focus of the Bali meetings was what to do after 2012, when the Kyoto Protocol expires.

International negotiations over how to achieve emissions reductions beyond 2012 began in 2005, when COP 11 met in Montreal, to mark the entry into force of the Kyoto Protocol. But the celebration didn't last long. By the time of the COP 13 meetings in Bali there was overwhelming new scientific evidence that global warming could be happening even faster than we had feared. The gap between Kyoto's proposed emissions reduction and the rapid global increase in carbon emissions had increased. This prompted a renewed sense of urgency to the climate negotiations.

The COP 13 meetings in Bali culminated in the 'Bali Roadmap', which launched the new negotiation process to determine Kyoto's successor. The roadmap insured at least two more years of talks before the process will be completed at the COP 15 meeting in 2009 in Copenhagen. The process may determine for years to come how the world will reduce emissions of greenhouse gases. We have little time left. The fate of the planet will be determined at Copenhagen in 2009.

An Insider's Account of the Bali Negotiations

Graciela Chichilnisky was a participant at the Bali climate negotiations event. This is her account of the event.

For me, Bali had the usual circus atmosphere of the United Nations Climate Convention events but this time in an exquisite setting. I was invited to participate in a side event by Hernan Carlino, the Chairman of the Clean Development Accreditation Committee and the representative of the group of developing nations (G77) in the Executive Committee of the Kyoto Protocol. My role was to present a proposal for a follow-up to the Kyoto Protocol after 2012.

The weather was warm and clear. The debates were, as usual, highly technical and this time the meetings were televised and viewed by the millions of people around the world who care about the future of Kyoto.

Yet by all accounts, the frustration of most negotiators at the meetings was palpable. At a time when most countries were ready to make a firm agreement about next steps, the US delegation insisted that more talk and debate was needed. The tension finally erupted in a David and Goliath-style show-down when the representative from Papua New Guinea, Kevin Conrad, boldly proclaimed to the US, in a televised statement that sent shockwaves around the world, '... I would ask the United States, we ask for your leadership, we seek your leadership, but if for some reason you are not comfortable leading, leave it to the rest of us, please get out.'[1]

Papua New Guinea is a small traditional nation with a large agenda: the preservation of their forests and their biodiversity. Despite appearances to the contrary, this nation is actually rather favourable and friendly towards the US. Until this point in the negotiations at Bali, the US had been, as usual, resistive and less than cooperative. After so many years of US hostility to the negotiations, many nations naturally wished that the US representative was not there in the first place, so as to allow others to move on with the agenda. Not so Papua New Guinea. After its bold statement, which was actually intended to bring the US back into the fold, the US made a surprising about-face and agreed to join the initiative to negotiate a follow-up agreement to Kyoto – the Bali Roadmap. To the world's surprise, the government of US President George W. Bush, one of the most resistant and hostile to environmental concerns in US history, agreed to follow the Bali Roadmap with the aim of joining the Kyoto Process at the end of 2009. This was a historic moment, misunderstood perhaps, but full of hope for change. Time will tell.

The meetings in Bali and the Bali Roadmap launched a new two-year negotiation process to tackle climate change. Like the 1996 Berlin Mandate that paved the way for the Kyoto Protocol, the Bali Roadmap is an agreement to agree. It ensures that the global community will embark on at least two more years of negotiation towards fashioning a successor to the Kyoto Protocol. The process should be completed at the COP 15 meeting in Copenhagen at the end of 2009.

Kyoto's future has never been more uncertain. At the April 2008 Bangkok meetings the EU, as discussed on p112, threw a spanner into the negotiations that marked the start of the Bali Roadmap. A failure of the Bali process could effectively terminate Kyoto. This reveals the uncertainty of the Kyoto Protocol's future.

We have barely set out on the road and already negotiations have stalled. Helping poor nations chart a new clean path to industrialization is central to the climate talks. But the atmosphere of the climate negotiations is not good. The conflict we face is clear: it is once again a global conflict between the rich and the poor nations, but in my view this conflict is created by a lack of understanding of what Kyoto can achieve, and how. In reality it can unify the interests of both.

Bali COP 13 was a larger meeting than ever. Non-governmental organizations (NGOs) made up the majority of the participants. At the meetings many dedicated environmentalists carried signs with dire predictions about the future of humankind and offering good omens to Kyoto. Dr Robert Watson, the former Chairman of the

Intergovernmental Panel on Climate Change (IPCC) was there, as was Professor Robert Stavins of Harvard University, who organized a well-advertised and attended side event on 'Kyoto after 2012' – the same topic as my own presentation in Bali, eliciting the participants' proposals on what to do about Kyoto but without making any proposals himself. In response to a question he made to the audience I asked for his own view of what to do but he offered no response.

New Proposals for the Post-Kyoto Regime

In this context, I presented my proposals at a panel together with Professor Peter Eisenberger of Columbia University and Professor Hernan Carlino of the UNFCCC. The panel was not well advertised and there were not many people in the room, but the participants were keen and intense and the presentations were officially recorded for posterity. Our presentations highlighted a proposal for the post-2012 Kyoto regime in two parts. The first part was a new type of negative carbon technology that we proposed ought to be incorporated as part of the Kyoto Protocol's Clean Development Mechanism (CDM). We argued that the technology, which is based on capturing carbon from air, was needed to prevent global warming in a timely fashion and could help poor nations; they can capture more carbon than they emit, thus attracting credits from the Kyoto Protocol. The second part of the proposal involved a global financial mechanism that builds on the carbon market itself, and can potentially resolve the China–US impasse.[2]

The two proposals can resolve the core of the conflict between poor and rich nations and the most important obstacles that Kyoto faces today. However, we are engaged in a race against time. Change takes place slowly at the international level and we may not have the time needed for a process of this nature to reach fruition.

The technology we proposed reduces atmospheric carbon while producing electricity. It uses the same energy for both processes, so it 'cogenerates' carbon reduction and electricity production. This unusual technology can greatly accelerate the reduction of carbon from the planet's atmosphere as required by IPCC targets, while at the same time increasing the production of energy in the world. This one–two punch of more energy and less carbon seems an almost impossible combination to many people. It appears almost too good to be true. Yet it is, in reality, the latest generation of a tried-and-tested technology called Carbon Capture and Sequestration (CCS), which has been in operation since 1996, was recently the subject of a McKinsey & Company report in the EU[3] and is widely accepted as part of the future.

CCS methods have been used for over 13 years by the oil industry to 'scrub' carbon from its production process, and inject it into oil deposits to enhance oil recovery, which it does by as much as 30–40 per cent.[4] The following sites have been successfully operating CCS for several years and each captures about 1 million tons of carbon dioxide a year: Sleipner, Norway (offshore) since 1996; Weyburn, Canada, since 2000; Salah, Algeria, since 2004 and Snovit, Norway, since 2008. The best that can be achieved with this conventional CCS process is 'carbon neutrality', namely to clean up all the carbon that the plant emits, and no more. However, we propose a different approach, a new generation CCS that is 'carbon negative' rather than 'carbon neutral', by extracting carbon directly from the atmosphere. The American Physics Society (APS) is at the time of writing producing a report on this new technology.[5] This negative carbon approach is drastically different and more effective than the carbon neutral method because it actually reduces the concentration of carbon from the atmosphere in the process of producing electricity.

The properties of this new technology are surprising to many and Hernan Carlino thought it would be important to bring a discussion of them forward in the context of the Bali COP, when the future of the Kyoto Protocol would be discussed. We had discussed the technology a year earlier in August 2006 in Buenos Aires, Argentina, where I was giving several presentations and touring Patagonia with its spectacular whales and huge – now melting – glaciers. We decided at the time that negative carbon technologies could benefit from the funding provided by the Kyoto Protocol Clean Development Mechanism (CDM) for clean energy. For this we only needed to modify the CDM to accept it. The technology is best suited to developing nations that do not emit much carbon such as the African or Latin American nations because negative carbon allows them to capture more carbon than they emit, which is very little. This way these nations can sell a substantive amount of carbon credits in the carbon market. For example, Africa currently emits about 3 per cent of global emissions and, under current CDM practices, has little carbon emissions to reduce and therefore little to sell in terms of carbon credits. For this reason most of the CDM funding for clean projects (over $23 billion so far) goes today to the developing nations that emit most carbon – such as China. Using negative carbon processes, such as carbon capture from air, algae's capture of carbon, etc., Africa could capture for example 20 per cent of world emissions, even though it only emits 3 per cent. The carbon it captures could be sold in the carbon market, benefitting Africa commercially as well as reducing the world's carbon concentration in the atmosphere. In addition, if the negative carbon technologies can augment Africa's energy production – by cogenerating electricity and carbon capture as mentioned above – then there is a triple benefit for Africa and for the world: Africa can develop more energy plants and sell more carbon credits in the carbon markets, enhancing African development – and the rest of the world can benefit from lower carbon levels in the atmosphere as well as from exporting technology to Africa for its new cogeneration plants. It is a truly remarkable and completely realistic possibility all round and at $15 billion per year of CDM investments today, the CDM could do a world of good to developing nations. The inexpensive and clean energy generated in these negative carbon projects would allow development in Africa and Latin America as nothing has done before. Development is all about energy. Reciprocally, by making the Kyoto targets easier to achieve, this technology can make Kyoto targets more realistic and thus supports the Protocol's continuation into the future. It is a win-win approach.

My second proposal at the Bali event was even more audacious than the first. It also went to the core of the conflicts between the poor and the rich nations that continue to stall the negotiations. This second proposal is to introduce a new global financial mechanism as part of the post-2012 Kyoto Protocol that builds on the carbon market that I proposed in the early 1990s and became part of the Kyoto Protocol in 1997. This new mechanism is specifically designed to overcome the China–US impasse. For all intents and purposes, the proposed mechanism would perform as a way to introduce limits on Chinese and other developing nations' emissions without, however, contradicting Article 4 of the UN Climate Convention. It would provide assurances to the US and would at the same time compensate China for carbon reductions. The proposed financial mechanism would replicate in financial terms almost exactly the wording of Article 4 of the 1992 Climate Convention of the United Nations (see p56). I had presented this proposal at the International Monetary Fund in Washington DC twice in August and also in October 2007. On each occasion it received a very favourable if somewhat startled reception. My official presentation at the Bali COP, in December 2007, was received with the same combination of interest and surprise.

In the ensuing months, Hernan Carlino would leave his position at the CDM Committee. Yet the discussions continued, and I presented the proposals on 12 November 2008 to the Australian Parliament in Victoria at a briefing organized by MP Michael Crutchfield, receiving an enthusiastic response, and to prominent Australian businessmen. This led to a request for another briefing with their Minister of the Environment Gavin Jennings and with the Ministry of Primary Industries and its Deputy Secretary Dale Seymour, towards the creation of a demonstration plant for this technology at Gypsland Victoria, home of the largest brown coal deposits in the world.

'Et tu Brute?'

The negotiation process is long and arduous, and only after the fact does it becomes clear whether a particular event is a failure or a success. The Bali Roadmap process will develop throughout 2009, and we will only know its results in November and December 2009. But it has significant obstacles to overcome.

The Kyoto Protocol is an important first step toward the UNFCCC goal of a low-carbon global economy that provides for basic needs while respecting ecological limits. Yet, despite this, the budding Kyoto Protocol may already be on its last legs just a few years after it came into force. This time, however, the threat comes from an unlikely enemy. Recent European proposals, supported by Japan, could destroy what Kyoto has already accomplished and its promise for the future. The EU and Japan have been the strongest and most loyal supports of global climate negotiations so far, so why now are they suddenly changing their course?

The challenge is an old threat with a new face. In April 2008 European negotiators went into a United Nations climate meeting in Bangkok. They warned the representatives of developing countries that they needed to step up to the challenge of climate change if they were to see additional money flowing into CDM projects in their countries. Their words seem reasonable; we all need to step up to the challenge of climate change. But the reality behind the words is badly wrong, alarmingly so. What the EU proposes reverses the one policy that can most effectively step up to the challenge of climate change.

The EU proposes to cap investment through the CDM, investments that are profitable for industrial nations' businesses and that create clean technologies in developing nations. These investments prepare the world for a future with fewer emissions, beginning with nations that are projected to be the largest emitters in the future. If successful in limiting the CDM, the EU will succeed in dismantling an important tool for future emission reductions.

The recommendations in Bangkok reflect a misunderstanding of what Kyoto intended, and what in fact, Kyoto has already achieved. The recommendations by the EU were intended to boost emissions reductions at home in Europe, while giving 'developing nations incentives to do more than sit back and watch the money flow.'[6] But increasing investment for clean technologies to developing nations is an important part of what the CDM has achieved thus far. The purpose of the CDM goes beyond just transferring money to developing nations – although this could be considered a worthwhile goal on its own. The purpose of the CDM is to create hard-earned and profitable projects that will transform development in the poorest nations into a new kind of clean development. By design, the CDM is intended to enable developing countries to move into a new type of industrialization that the world badly needs.

There is increasing recognition that industrialized nations, who are most responsible for climate change, cannot adequately address the climate crisis alone, given the rapid rise in emissions in emerging economies. But in a somewhat perverse response to the problem, the European Commission proposed a set of policy proposals that would scale back the CDM, the only mechanism under the Kyoto Protocol that provides incentives for reducing emissions in developing nations. The EU proposals would essentially cap the CDM at current levels until 2020 if a new climate treaty is not reached. Commission officials say that a moderate expansion would be allowed if an agreement in Copenhagen is reached, although estimates vary as to the actual impact.

But looking beyond the strategic errors and misunderstandings, the European Commission has an important point. The CDM programme is in need of reform. Indeed, it may not be the right model to solve many problems unless and until it is reformed, which can be achieved with modest changes. For instance, developers are now requesting new CDM credits for hydroelectric, wind power and, most recently, natural gas-fired power plants in China. There is some perversity in the CDM programme if 60 per cent of all CDM projects fund changes in China's energy structure, while the poorest nations in the world are left out because they emit so little and so cannot reduce their emissions significantly.

As previously discussed, CDM projects must be carefully monitored to guarantee that offsets represent verifiable emissions reductions above and beyond business-as-usual baselines. This monitoring is done by the UNFCCC Kyoto Protocol Accreditation Committee, but it is a bureaucracy that requires streamlining to make it possible for small and poor nations, such as Bolivia and Mongolia, with little or no investment banking know-how, to compete for CDM projects.

Despite these known problems with the CDM, problems that can be successfully addressed, the logic of the new EU proposal is flawed. It is so flawed that it has created strange bedfellows – the poorest nations of the world and the rich nations' businesses. Poor countries fear that the proposal will dry up the steady flow of funding for investment in clean technologies that was available since 2005, while businesses fear that the recent proposals will throw the entire carbon-offset industry, currently valued at $50 billion, into flux.[7] 'The cap on clean development projects proposed by the EU, as it is designed now, will not provide any incentive for people to design new (clean technology) projects. Effectively the market will be killed.' So says Michaela Beltracchi, European Policy Coordinator for the International Emissions Trading Association, based in Geneva, Switzerland, which represents a range of business interests.[8]

European nations have not done enough to ready themselves for a carbon-neutral future. They may very well fail to achieve their committed Kyoto targets by 2012. Italy, for example, is registering emissions growth of 13 per cent, when it is supposed to meet an emissions cap of 6.5 per cent.[9] But the CDM is not to blame. One widely acknowledged problem is that the EU set too lenient limits on carbon emissions as part of its own internal cap-and-trade program. This depressed the price of carbon permits in the EU carbon market, and provided less incentive for industry to invest in emission reductions within the EU. Their experience is now hailed as an example of what not to do with cap-and-trade. In the US the emerging consensus is that carbon allowances must be sold, perhaps in public auctions, to emitters. This is not only fair but efficient. But there are political pressures mounting in the US against the carbon market and its CDM. Will these forces prevail in the US as they did in Europe?

The Present vs the Future

In the current debate there are two powerful opposing points of view. One represents the past and the other represents the future. Advocates of the Kyoto Protocol represent the future and they face steady criticism that the carbon market is not really reducing emissions but that it is merely transferring wealth to developing nations. Critics argue that most of the emissions reduction projects in the CDM would have proceeded anyway, therefore they do not represent additional reductions above and beyond business as usual. Along the same lines, critics have argued that the CDM may not be as credible as it should be and that we need to take those concerns seriously.[10]

The EU is especially concerned that Europe itself needs to spur more technologies now, and that paying for offsets elsewhere doesn't prompt the technological innovation the EU needs to solve the problem. Others believe that pulling the plug on the CDM will have little effect on the climate talks. They believe that the CDM could go and China would not even notice.[11] All the CDM projects in China, which are about 60 per cent of the entire CDM project base, represent less than 1 per cent of the country's annual growth.

In a startling about-face, business interests are now working themselves to preserve and expand the CDM. This is just as the EU Commission's proposal against it moves through the European Parliament this year to curtail the CDM. One proposal is to leave the overall cap on European emissions in place and reduce international caps in all nations. This would ensure that investments in new technologies are made at home while allowing the CDM to grow and expand.

Another big question for the future is how international CDM credits will be handled by the United States, whose carbon market could dwarf the European Union's. The leading climate negotiations in the US Senate could limit international offsets to 15 per cent of the overall market. Critics suggest that the US legislation could allow other nations to 'launder' international credits with no oversight from the US, so the US would have little or no effect on an important international debate.

But the US itself is involved in another major global conflict: the competition for resources by rich nations, in this case the US, and poor nations, in this case China. This conflict manifests itself here in the US's refusal to ratify the Kyoto Protocol and therefore participate in the carbon market altogether, unless China accepts some limits on its own emissions. The uncertain future of the Kyoto Protocol is created by the current China–US Impasse, which is truly dramatic. This is first-class global politics. The competition is between an old superpower and a new superpower. It is the oldest type of competition there is and the world's climate is hostage to its resolution.

The issue is now in the realm of global geopolitics at the largest possible scale. It is the new geopolitics of the 21st century. Rich and poor nations are no longer competing for nuclear power as they did during the cold war era, although the risks and rewards of nuclear power have not gone away. They are now competing for natural resources and, in the case of global climate change, they are competing for user rights to the atmospheric commons.

Yet the nations of the world have a new terrifying and unifying risk to contend with: global warming. The similarity with nuclear risks is not idle. As in the case of nuclear power, the risks we face can unify us, precisely because they are so large and potentially catastrophic; because the survival of the species may be at stake. This is an unexpected silver lining in the global warming cloud: global warming has a capability for unifying the human race like nothing has done before.

For the first time in history we truly are all in the same boat. For the first time, poor nations are in a position to have a major impact on the standards of living, even the survival, of rich nations. African nations, simply by growing their economies through their own energy resources, coal and petroleum, have the ability to incur trillions of dollars in losses for the US. The OECD reports that Miami is at risk of $3.5 trillion in property damages if African countries induce a rapid increase in the sea level, simply by burning their own coal and oil.[12] Until now a US citizen could be concerned about the standard of living of African people but not have a direct self-interest in the matter of how African nations grow their economies. This is certainly the first time in history that we can say that African countries have the power to considerably reduce the standard of living in the US. It sounds very bad. But in reality it is the opposite. Now the US has a real, bona fide self-interest in the clean development of African nations. And the same is true about the clean development of Latin America. These are the two geographical areas from where the US imports most of its fossil fuels and natural resources as a whole. As with all risk, there is always opportunity.

Rich or Poor: Who Should Abate Emissions?

We all know that developing nations hold the key to the future. They will become the large emitters as they industrialize. Today they make up a mere 40 per cent of global emissions, but they could emit the majority in 20 or 30 years. To avoid this they need to follow a clean path to industrialization, something that is not apparent to the eye today as we observe China building one out of every two of the world's new coal power plants every week.[13]

The issue is how to ensure a clean future for the poor nations of today. One way that is widely discussed is whether or not to cap developing nations' emissions. This is specifically forbidden in Article 4 of the 1992 United Nations Framework Convention on Climate Change (UNFCC), which states that unless developing nations are compensated they will not be required to reduce emissions. The issue is so controversial that it can be called the 'third rail' in international climate debates. If the issue is not resolved, as it must be in Copenhagen, negotiations could break down without an agreement for what should follow the Kyoto Protocol in 2012. The US has already stated its unwillingness to accept limits on its greenhouse gas emissions unless China accepts the same. But now they are joined in the call for capping developing countries' emissions by the EU. The EU has recently said that developing nations should accept caps of 15–30 per cent of their business as usual emissions.[14]

What crucial decisions have to be made in Copenhagen to save Kyoto? First, the nations have to agree to reduce the global cap on emissions. The Kyoto Protocol mandates an average emissions reduction of 5.2 per cent of 1990 levels. So far this excludes the US and so the Protocol accounts for only part of the emissions from the industrialized world. This is a good start, but it is not enough. The Kyoto Protocol will not, by itself, reduce atmospheric warming appreciably. Further emission reductions will need to take place after the first commitment period. To avoid major climate disruption the IPCC urges an 80 per cent cut in emissions within 20 to 30 years. The international community understands the need for a lower emissions cap; what it does not agree on is how to reach it. Do we increase the caps for developed countries? Do we impose caps on developing countries?

Warming Up to Climate Action

One thing is clear: we can't reach the lower levels without US participation. On this front, things may not be nearly as bad as they were before. The US is the world's largest emitter – about 25 per cent of the world's emissions come from the US – and the USA has been the strongest opposition to the Kyoto Protocol. Yet things are changing; hundreds of US cities and towns have signed petitions demanding that the federal government in Washington ratify the Kyoto Protocol and join the carbon market. In 2007, the US Supreme Court agreed that the US Clean Air Act of 1963 gives the federal government the authority to regulate and limit greenhouse gas emissions.

Since the US abandoned the Kyoto Protocol in 2001, climate policy has slowly but surely advanced at regional, state and local levels within the US. The Regional Greenhouse Gas Initiative (RGGI), a collaborative effort of 10 northeastern and mid-Atlantic states, has mandated a 10 per cent cap on carbon emissions from the power sector by 2018. This is the first mandatory, market-based effort in the United States to reduce greenhouse gas emissions. Permits will be auctioned and revenues will be invested in energy efficiency, renewable and other clean technology projects. The Western Climate Initiative, which involves seven western states and four Canadian provinces, is moving towards the creation of its own regional cap-and-trade programme. These two regional initiatives could allow some US states to join the carbon market. In addition, the first federal climate policy initiative, the Lieberman Warner Climate Security Act, reached Congress in the spring of 2008. It too was based on a cap-and-trade system for emissions reduction and although it was defeated across Republican and Democratic Party lines, it set the stage for further negotiation over climate policy.

President Barack Obama acknowledges the urgency of the climate crisis and has called for national action to combat climate change. In particular, he has announced his support for moving the US back into the Kyoto Protocol. Environmental organizations across the US are geared up for a national cap-and-trade programme and expect ratification of the Kyoto Protocol.

Business interests in the US, the bastion of innovative capitalism, have warmed to climate policy as well. Silicon Valley Venture Capital is already investing 18 per cent of its risk capital in clean energy projects, and it is believed that this will increase rapidly when (or if) the US ratifies the Protocol. Analysts in major investment banks, such as JP Morgan Chase, now routinely use carbon footprinting to evaluate a company's risk profile. Business interests acknowledge that the US automobile industry is handicapped from benefitting from the 'price signal' of the carbon market that helps orient industry elsewhere to build vehicles with lower carbon emissions. For the first time, Toyota has replaced GM as the largest automobile maker in the world and the entire industry is in a state of crisis.

The US seems more firmly committed now than it was in 1997 to a market-based approach to emissions reduction. Australia, who along with the US represented the most recalcitrant opposition to the Protocol, has recently made its own turnaround. It ratified the Protocol in 2007 and this year has agreed to create its own internal carbon market as of 2010.[15]

This suggests that greater flexibility and further development of the global carbon market will be a pre-condition for the US to return. At the same time, the US will likely argue for caps on developing nations' emissions, especially China's and India's, to protect its industries from what it views as unfair competition on the basis of differential emissions standards. This will be the most difficult hurdle for negotiators to overcome in Copenhagen.

China is protected by the 1992 Convention Article 4 from accepting emissions limits unless it is compensated for emissions reductions. Once again, the CDM is the tool to overcome the problem, since with the CDM China can be compensated for reducing emissions as the Convention mandates. This is the seed of a solution.

To Cap or Not to Cap: That is the Question

The policy of rich nations towards poor nations is essential to the climate negotiations. It is the foundation of the CDM, which unifies the interests of businesses in the rich nations with the interests of poor nations in clean development. This community of interest between the North and the South, and the importance of the role of developing nations, is grounded in the Climate Convention of 1992. It is in fact, memorialized in its Article 4. The idea is that developing nations should be able to increase emissions for a time to grow their economies and lift their citizens out of poverty. The UN reports that over 50 per cent of the people in the world live on less than $2 per day, and 1.4 billion people live on the brink of survival, with income of less than $1.25 per day.[16] The developing nations export most of the fossil fuels that are used in the world but they neither use most of the fossil fuels nor produce most of the world emissions. Latin America and Africa are the main resource exporters in the world economy. They have exported their resources at prices that are so low that poverty has taken grip of their people and the rich nations have become 'addicted' to their fossil fuels and other resources.

The poor nations hardly consume energy at all. Consequently they produce very few emissions, about 40 per cent of the world's carbon. These nations are not the main cause of the global warming problem. Nor can they be the solution. But, in reality, poor nations are the main victims of global warming risks. Over 80 per cent of the planet lives in the developing world where we will see the worst consequences of global warming: desertification, agricultural losses, interruption of water supplies and terrifying exposure to rising sea levels.[17]

So it makes sense that the Kyoto Protocol granted developing countries unlimited user rights to the global atmospheric commons on equity grounds. But it was much easier to make this concession in 1997 than it is now. Energy consumption and emissions production in the developing world was so low that these countries offered little potential for emissions reduction. Because poor countries didn't emit much in the first place, it was obvious that developed nations had to shoulder the burden of global emissions reduction. Even today, the developing world only produces 40 per cent of global emissions. But that is rapidly changing.

The good news is that developing nations are growing – some much faster than others, and none with any guarantee that growth will trickle down to their poorest – but growing nonetheless. The bad news is that developing nations are growing – and consuming more energy in the process. There is a clear and direct connection between energy use and economic output. A country's industrial production can be measured from its use of energy.[18] Emissions from developing nations are increasing at a growing rate. The emissions growth rate in the developing world is higher, on average, than it is for all other countries, including the US. In the US carbon dioxide emissions are projected to increase at an average annual rate of 1.1 per cent from 2004 to 2030. Emissions from developing nation economies are projected to grow by 2.6 per cent per year.[19] As a result, developing countries' share of global emissions will rise. China could soon surpass the US as the world's largest emissions producer. This is all very persuasive evidence for the need to cap emissions growth in developing nations.

But there are equally persuasive arguments for not imposing emissions caps on low income countries. Global income inequality is more acute now than it has ever been in human history. Inequality between nations is larger than inequality found within any single country, including Brazil, South Africa and the US, where income inequality is known to be high. The top 5 per cent of people in the world receive about one-third of total world income. The top 10 per cent of people in the world receive one-half of the world's income. The ratio between the average income of the richest 5 per cent and the poorest 5 per cent of the world is 165 to 1. Roughly 70 per cent of global inequality can be explained by differences in countries' average incomes.[20] This means that to tackle the global divide we need to increase income growth in the poorest nations. This is much harder to do in a carbon-constrained world unless we can manage two things. First, energy consumption and emissions will have to increase in the developing world, at least in the short term, until we can develop and transfer technologies for renewable and clean energy resources and greater energy efficiency. Second, we have to reduce emissions in the developed world to a greater extent.

What About China?

What about China? Should China be treated differently? It's tempting to treat China, and India to some extent, as distinct from the rest of the developing world when it comes to global climate control. Indeed there are some important differences. China's annual economic growth rate trumps the growth rate of all other economies worldwide. China is now the sixth largest economy in the world. But with a population of 1.3 billion people, most of whom live in China's impoverished rural areas, per capita income in China still is only $2,360. In the US, per capita income is $46,040.[21] Disparities this large still warrant attention.

China adopted massive energy policy reforms over the last two decades aimed at increasing energy efficiency and conservation. Between 1997 and 2000, China reduced its emissions by 19 per cent, while its economy grew by 15 per cent.[22] China's sweeping measures represent emissions savings nearly equivalent to the entire US transportation sector.[23] But it is not only China that has taken such large voluntary steps forward to reduce or slow the growth of their emissions. For example, both Indonesia and China are phasing out fossil fuel subsidies. China, Mexico, Thailand and the Philippines have established national goals for renewable energy use and energy efficiency. Argentina and India are converting automobiles and public transport to natural gas.[24] The Costa Rican government recently announced its goal of making the country carbon neutral over the next 10 to 15 years.

In comparison, emissions in the US continue to rise. US initiatives aimed at reducing greenhouse gases have been mostly voluntary and not well-coordinated across the country. Most US passenger vehicles could not now be driven in China, where fuel-efficiency standards are higher. It is hard to expect developing countries to implement binding limits on their greenhouse gas emissions when the wealthiest of the industrialized nations is unwilling to follow suit.

Yet at the same time, the recent news coming from China is a source of concern. Although it can still boast much lower per capita emissions that the rich nations of the world, the Chinese Academy of Sciences now reports that China's aggregate emissions will tower above all other countries in the world, including the US, much sooner than anyone had anticipated.[25] This news increases the pressure on China to accept caps in the next round of negotiations in Copenhagen. It also indicates the enormous challenge China will face meeting any emissions target. Acknowledging the need to cap China's emissions is only the first step and taking that step will be an uphill battle. But demonstrating the capacity of China to meet such a cap may be even harder. This is where the carbon market can help; it can channel investment into emissions reduction where the world needs it most – in China.

The current conflict between the US and China has plagued climate negotiations since their beginnings. More generally, the conflict between the rich and the poor nations is the cause of Kyoto's uncertain future. Why?

What is at stake in the global negotiations is fundamentally a question of who has the right to use the world's resources today and in the future, the rich or the poor nations. We know who used the resources in the past, the rich nations, and this is how they industrialized. The developing nations rightly feel that rich nations are now trying to kick away the ladder that they used to climb to their industrialization heights, preventing 80 per cent of the world from joining them. Furthermore, the poor nations feel they are being asked to solve an emissions problem that was created by the industrial nations, the same nations who bought their natural resources too inexpensively in the first place.

How can poor countries pursue their economic development without jeopardizing the future for us all? We need to encourage and assist developing countries to embark on a greener, more carbon-neutral path to prosperity than the one rich countries followed during their industrialization. In all cases, we need to preserve and expand Kyoto's global carbon market, because it sets a market approach to achieve a new form of clean industrialization.

The global carbon market must be carefully regulated to ensure an appropriate global cap on emissions and transparent trading. But once this is achieved, it can provide powerful incentives to developing countries to reduce emissions, without resorting to caps.

It effectively imposes a price on their carbon emissions, a price that they still have the flexibility not to pay, but at a cost.

Without caps, developing countries could produce greenhouse gases with impunity but they could gain more from limiting emissions and selling credits through the CDM. In effect this means that developing countries still incur a 'price' for their emissions. Every tonne of emission they produce represents a tonne of emissions reduction they could have sold at the prevailing world price for carbon reduction. Economists have a special name for this: opportunity cost. The opportunity cost of generating emissions when you could have sold emissions reduction credits to industrialized countries is in itself a powerful incentive not to emit.

This is a very different incentive structure than what existed for all nations prior to the Kyoto Protocol; a time when all emissions were essentially un-priced and unaccounted for in decision-making. In summary: thanks to the CDM, developing countries face an incentive to reduce their emissions, even without caps.

And yet we still have not fully utilized the CDM, a potent feature of the Kyoto Protocol. The demand for buying emissions reduction credits through the CDM is less than its potential. The market is new and the learning curve for buying and selling in this market is steep. The cost of starting a CDM project is high and must be decreased. At present the costs are prohibitively high both in terms of cash and of know-how, for all but the largest projects. Time and improved streamlining of the costs of applying for CDM project certification can fix this part of the problem. But as long as the EU limits the use of the CDM, by maintaining that developed countries must meet most of their emissions reduction commitment 'at home', the demand for these credits and the price developing countries can be paid for these credits will be less than its potential.

We can increase the demand for CDM projects, and facilitate a greater transfer of technologies and capital to developing countries, by imposing more stringent caps on industrialized country emissions. To the extent that an expanded global carbon market can provide developed countries with greater flexibility, lower mitigation costs transfer of technology and more energy for development, it makes it easier to convince industrialized countries to accept lower emission caps for the future.

The carbon market saved the Kyoto Protocol once, by providing a mechanism for uniting the interests of poor and rich nations. Can we do it all over again in Copenhagen 2009? The proposals on negative carbon and new financial mechanisms discussed above could save the day. But it is a race against time.

North–South: An Uncertain Future

International trade, particularly between rich and poor nations, has come under intense scrutiny in recent years. Many acknowledge that international trade benefits rich countries more than poor countries. Why are we so confident that the carbon market will be any different?

Trade is often credited with increasing economic growth. A country's economic growth is measured by its Gross Domestic Product (GDP), a measure of the market value of all of the goods and services it produces over a given year. Growth leads to more resource consumption and more use of the atmosphere. Yet GDP does not account for all of the harmful effects of our production and consumption. For example, the increased threat of climate risk associated with emissions production is not reflected in fossil fuel prices or in the prices of goods and services produced with fossil fuels in the economy. Today, spending to clean up an environmental disaster, such as an oil spill, contributes positively toward GDP, since it creates demand for goods and services related to mitigation. For these reasons as well as others, it is now widely accepted that GDP is not the best indicator of the health and sustainability of an economy or the well-being of the people that the economy supports. The carbon market creates prices that help redress this problem.

A reasonable question is how can markets that trade emissions rights help the environment, markets that are implicated in creating the global environmental problem we face today? How can a market solution correct a market problem? We must rethink our assumptions: environment and markets need not always be at odds.

GDP growth isn't a global villain but neither is it the best index of economic success. In recognition of this, the United Nations is revising its measures of economic growth and systems of national accounts. Since the turn of the 21st century, the United Nations' Millennium Goals Programme monitors the satisfaction of basic needs across the world – further recognition that other measures of progress are needed beyond GDP.

GDP growth is not synonymous with progress, especially where the environment is concerned. But there is an important link between poverty and environmental degradation, which can be traced to false interpretations of what constitutes a nation's comparative advantage. Because GDP, and market prices more generally, ignore the environmental costs of economic activity, it improperly signals what countries should specialize and trade in, within the global marketplace. Countries may appear able to provide goods and services at comparatively lower costs, but this is only because market prices ignore the environmental and social costs of the production. It is this mis-signalling of what countries should specialize in and produce for the global economy that leads to over-exploitation of resources and poverty. It is at the heart of the global warming crisis.

The way we measure economic progress using GDP is particularly flawed for developing nations. It is inappropriate, because developing nations treat their natural resources, be they forests, fisheries, fresh water supplies or mineral deposits, as common property resources. As common property resources, these countries cannot restrict access to these resources or protect them from over-use. The price for using these resources neither reflects their underlying scarcity, the damage that is caused by the processes of extracting them or the loss of ecosystem services or values when they are removed from natural systems in unsustainable ways. What this means is that the price for these resources in developing countries is inappropriately cheap. This gives the false impression of a comparative advantage and it leads poor nations to specialize in exporting resources. As shown by Chichilnisky in 1994, this leads to a skewed pattern of trade between the North and the South, where the South exports natural resources to the North at very low prices, which in turn leads to over-consumption of resources across the world.[26]

Over the last 40 years, even as the United Nations (UN) community enthusiastically adopted basic needs as the central goal of sustainable development at the 1992 Earth Summit, the world economy increased its momentum in exactly the opposite direction. This unfortunate trend confirmed the worse predictions about the impacts of resource trade on poverty and on the world's resources. Today, 1.2 billion people live below the threshold of meeting basic needs. As a result we have rapidly magnified the use of natural resources around the world, particularly in developing nations, and we have also magnified world poverty. Both results are driven by an unsustainable model of economic growth based on GDP that encourages increasing amounts of resource exports by developing nations at prices that are often below replacement costs.

Recent empirical work has shown that current measures of GDP increase as developing nations open their economies to trade, most of which is trade in natural resources. This work also shows how opening up an economy to trade inevitably increases the inequality of income within the exporting nation, undermining economic growth – an unavoidable connection that was established and predicted way back in 1979.[27]

It has been shown that what matters most is what the nation trades.[28] Exporting raw materials or labour-intensive products does not help countries to move out of poverty. Exporting capital-intensive or knowledge-intensive products, products that correspond to a higher level of development than the nation as a whole, is what makes export policies favourable for the nations, creating growth, wealth and overall progress. Poor countries, with their abundance of natural resources and low-skilled labour forces specialize in the former. Rich nations specialize in the latter. At present our global trade patterns – what countries specialize in – are destined to increase the global income divide. Can the global carbon market help reverse this? The answer is a qualified yes, as is shown below.

Today we can see the results of the export-led growth policies of the last 40 years, which are based on maximizing GDP, assumed false comparative advantages and over-represented the gains from trade, leading to more inequality and deprivation in the exporting nations.[29] Forty years later we face the worse environmental dilemmas in history and have the greatest ever number of poor people on the planet, both of which are caused by a runaway overuse of natural resources.

Clearly we must undo all this; we must redress the world's overuse of natural resources and the attendant runaway poverty and degradation in the developing world – the two problems are intimately connected. The whole situation appears to be a misunderstanding of gargantuan proportions, a cognitive dissonance between orthodox economic theory, history and practice. The carbon market prices help correct this monumental error.

Trade vs Environment: A False Choice

The traditional so-called trade-off between economic development and the environment does not exist. It is illusory at best, and deeply wrong and damaging at worst – it portrays a false choice. The entire issue of trade and the environment needs rethinking, because sustainable economic growth is actually consistent with sustainable trade strategies. Appropriate policies for trade and for the environment reinforce each other. A two-pronged approach can focus on the conceptual issues involved while offering at the same time practical policy recommendations. To be understood the concepts must be situated in the context of existing international agreements and perspectives within the industrial and developing nations. We need to describe how these came about in historic terms and how to move positively into the future.

After decades of using theories of economic development that encourage growth based on exports of resources, the two-way relationship, where trade is viewed as encroaching on the environment, and environmental issues on trade, came to the fore at the current trade negotiations of the World Trade Organization's (WTO) agreement, which began in 2001. Just like the conflicts between rich and poor countries over climate change, the process exposed profound differences in the perspectives, and even clashes of interest, between the rich industrialized and the developing nations. The clashes between the positions of the North and the South continue today. What is it about the trade and environment nexus that polarizes public opinion in such a way?

It must be understood that talking about the North and the South is a huge oversimplification. We see this in the current climate negotiations as well. The issue of whether to cap emissions in China is very different from the issue of whether to cap emissions in Kenya, Nicaragua or Laos. The North and the South are far from being large blocks defined by common interests. The US and EU continue to differ on fundamental issues of trade and the environment, such as agricultural subsidies, genetically modified organisms and – as is the subject of this book – the control of greenhouse gas emissions. Similarly, the South represents nations at different stages of development and different interests. Brazil is very different from Bolivia, Nigeria or Cameroon. China is very different from almost all other developing nations.

Even so, and particularly on issues related to the environment and trade and global warming, the North–South dichotomy continues to be relevant. It helps to understand the problems and to find solutions. Earlier in this chapter we gave a reason for this: the central issue, the core of the global environmental dilemma, is the way human societies around the world organize property rights and price natural resources.[30] This is the source of the global environmental problems we face. The conflict between trade and the environment also has the same origin, as shown by Chichilinsky in 1994 (see p62).

In the North, natural resources are generally held as private property and traded as such, while in the South they are held as common property. Resources – forests, water or oil – are often called the 'property of the people' in the South. This North–South difference is at the foundation of the entire environmental dilemma, as well as the source of the pattern of natural resource trade in the world economy.

The North–South pattern of trade is responsible for the worst environmental problem of our times. Global warming arises from overuse of fossil fuels and this in turn stems from extremely low fossil fuel prices. Global warming would not exist if fossil fuel prices were several times higher (in which case we would be using other available forms of energy). But low fossil fuel prices, determined directly by international markets, is what we have been used to. Oil is a global commodity and its price is a global issue. Petroleum has been very inexpensive in recent years (even today it is still relatively cheap despite the recent increases in prices) because it is exported from developing nations that price their natural resources too low. More realistic – namely, higher – market prices for oil could solve the problem. But nobody can tell a market what prices should be; markets have their own ways of determining prices. The price of oil within the global markets depends on the proper functioning of natural resource markets. In order for a market to reflect true costs it requires well-defined property rights on natural resources in the exporting nations – the developing nations.

What is of specific interest for us is that the connection between trade and the environment can be changed as it depends on global property rights on natural resources that are under consideration right now. The essence of the Kyoto Protocol is to assign property rights to the use of the planet's atmosphere. Furthermore, appropriate systems of property rights on global resources – biodiversity, the global airwaves, the planet's atmosphere and the water masses of the world – can be created at a global scale, and used as a practical tool for levelling the playing field between rich and poor. They can be used to design effective and policy-relevant solutions to the conflict between the two.

Before providing a property rights scheme that works at a global scale, it is worth pointing out that the positions of the North and the South on the issue of trade and development have changed dramatically over time. Traditionally, as we saw before, the South resisted liberalizing international trade for fear of the North's domination of the global markets. Almost paradoxically, over time the North and the South have shifted places, each taking the side previously held by the other. Initially the developing nations feared trade and liberalization, which could result in deforestation and poverty at the hands of powerful Northern governments, governments that represent the interests of large corporations and that are unwilling to honour their commitments in trade negotiations.

Currently, however, the developing nations tend to favour international trade more than the industrial nations. In the WTO developing nations now insist on free trade for their products, while industrial nations are often seen as protecting their markets, for agricultural products for example, and are against outsourcing. In that sense they view each other as antagonists. Labour in the North has found common cause with environmental groups who are concerned with Southern imports that result in deforestation, climate change, loss of biodiversity, species loss and other forms of environmental degradation.

While the Northern and Southern interests coincided in blocking many negotiations, there are important differences in perceptions on just who the villains and the heroes are. People in the North are often of the opinion that it is the international corporations, which put profits before people and engage cheap labour, thereby de-industrializing Southern goods and causing unemployment at home, who are the bad guys. For the environmentalists, it is careless Southern governments as much as greedy multinationals. And for Southern governments it is the powerful Northern governments.

The emphasis we give to the issue of property rights is not surprising. The issue of property rights is certainly not new, but what is different and new here is the emphasis on global property rights to resources, rather than the more familiar issues of national or local property rights to resources such as land reform. Indeed, issues of property rights have always played a key role in economic thinking. In the 20th century they were used to separate capitalism from socialism. Capitalism was seen as an economic system based on individual private property rights on the means of production – on capital – while socialism emphasized common or social property rights on capital. The two political systems, capitalism and socialism, differ precisely in their views of what is the best property rights regime for the inputs of production such as capital. Capitalism says capital should be private property, socialism says it should be owned as common property. All this is well known – the debate between capitalism and socialism is really somewhat dated and is not relevant to the environment.

The issue of property rights remains current today, albeit in a radically different way. The world economy can be best viewed today as divided, not into socialist and capitalistic nations, as it was in the early 20th century, but rather into the North and the South, the rich and the poor nations. The South is composed mostly of pre-industrial or agricultural economies, and the North of post-industrial economies. And in both types of economies capital is not the most relevant input to production; it is not the main issue. The issue is no longer 'who owns the capital?' Rather, 'who owns the natural resources?' and 'who owns knowledge?' The issue relevant for the global environment is the global property rights to global natural resources: which countries own the rights to the resources that will be critically important in sustaining future welfare. This changes the underlying premises of capitalism and socialism about who owns capital, and both capitalistic nations, such as the US, and socialist societies, such as China, face similar environmental dilemmas today.

Pressing Concerns

A sceptical reader may ask why this problem was not detected before, why is the issue of global property rights on resources emerging only now? The reason is simple and can be best seen by analogy. We did not worry about the property rights to use roads, namely traffic light systems, until there was enough traffic. The first settlers in America did not worry about the property rights to land – it was free until it became scarce. And we never worried about global rights to natural resources, the atmosphere of the planet, its water bodies and its biodiversity until human populations increased sufficiently to endanger these resources. In the entire history of our planet, human populations have never been so large: there are 6.7 billion people on the planet today and there are predicted to be 9 billion people by 2042. The population growth that we are experiencing now was unprecedented before the 20th century, and because the situation is relatively new, our historical institutions are ill prepared for the change. We lack global organizations to deal with the new global challenges. Now we urgently need to organize the global society in respect of its use of natural resources, just as we needed to organize our roads when traffic volume reached high levels. And for the same reason: to avoid unnecessary conflict and strife, costs, suffering and deaths. This is why global property rights on resources were not an issue until now.

Natural resources such as petroleum, water bodies and the atmosphere of the planet are today more important than capital in a global context. They determine the main economic issues of globalization and the attendant environmental risks, and the global conflict between trade and the environment. Capital is no longer the main input of production in advanced societies as it was in the industrial societies of the beginning of the 20th century. Nor is capital the main determinant of production and trade in developing nations. In pre-industrial economies, which we call the South, the property rights that matter are predominantly those used for owning and trading land and agricultural products and, more generally, those for owning and trading natural resources. Similarly, in the post-industrial economies that buy resources from the South, the main input of production is knowledge rather than capital. For these reasons, the explanations given here for the environmental and trade issues, and the solutions proposed for these issues, focus on a different type of property rights than those that were important at the beginning of the 20th century. Property rights on resources are more relevant in today's world that is divided between the North and the South.

In summary: the debate about the environment today is not over socialism or capitalism but rather between two other forms of economic organization – agricultural and post-industrial societies that are connected through international markets. The environmental dilemma cuts through and across conventional political divisions of left and right, capitalism and socialism. This has been confusing to many who persist in holding onto somewhat outdated left–right forms of thinking. Conserving the environment is important for both sides. The basic environmental issues we face are due to the fact that natural resources are exported and over-extracted in the South and are imported and over-consumed in the North. This is the relevant dichotomy that we must address if we want to understand and resolve the global environmental dilemmas of our times: global warming, ozone depletion and the destruction of the complex web of species that make life on earth. We must deal with the economic foundations of a market-based relationship between the North and the South.

The entire global environmental issue is the over-extraction and the over-consumption of natural resources across the world. The over-extraction of natural resources in the South leads to the over-consumption of these same resources in the North. At the end of the day this is what the global environmental problem is all about. Think of it this way: if the North significantly reduced imports of petroleum and the South significantly decreased oil production and and extraction of forest products, thereby allowing the number of forests in the world to significantly increase, then the global warming problem would not exist. It would disappear. And many other global environmental problems would be resolved or greatly improved. The majority of the world's biodiversity that is threatened with extinction today involves species that live mostly in the world's forests and the attendant surrounding areas and water bodies; they could be sustained if their ecosystems remained intact.

The process of using global property rights to resolve the issues of trade and environment has begun. Its beginnings were humble and it is largely misunderstood, but the process is so important that it begs for clarification – as do the policy tools that can accelerate its adoption and its use.

Global property rights on resources are the main ingredient and the most distinguishing feature of the Kyoto Protocol. The Protocol created a global system of property rights on natural resources that is necessary for our era of globalization.

International agreements such as the Kyoto Protocol, with its groundbreaking system of global property rights on the use of the atmosphere, hold the key to the future. They can resolve and harmonize the worse conflicts we face in the areas of trade and the environment. The Kyoto Protocol represents only a beginning; a template for what is to come. However if one could design the global economy today – to ensure a better future for billions of people on the planet – one could not do much better than to use this template as a blueprint of what is needed, of things to come.

The Kyoto Protocol is more than a system of allocations of property rights on the use of the atmosphere – who can emit what – and the trading of these rights among nations. It also contains an asymmetric treatment for the North and the South, for the poor and the rich nations. By purposeful design, this is a global market that is skewed in favour of what poor countries have to sell. They own most of the environmental resources in the world and they use these to sell CDM credits to industrial nations. This is a step in the right direction, both for the environment and for eliminating global inequality, that limits carbon emissions and helps resolve climate change. This is why the Kyoto Protocol's carbon market can pass the litmus test of even the most ardent market and trade sceptics. It deserves to be given a chance.

Saving Kyoto

6

The Kyoto Protocol is far from perfect, so why save it? Because it achieved something that is important for us all and most people thought was impossible: it capped global greenhouse gas emissions. It is the first time in our history that we have agreed to limit our carbon emissions and change our energy use, which is the only way to avert global warming. Not a small achievement.

Rather than reinventing the wheel, now we have to improve on what took us years to achieve. Let's save Kyoto! Time is short because we could be precipitating irreversible changes in weather patterns right now, as you read. There is no time to waste.

In all honesty, even if we wanted to reinvent the wheel and tried to negotiate yet another international agreement to reduce emissions from scratch, we would still need to follow the Kyoto route. Why? Because Kyoto and its carbon market have extraordinary features, features that are often misunderstood, that are critical for humankind.

What are these magical features? The basic feature is to cap global emissions. We mention three more and the reader can evaluate how truly magical they are: first of all, the carbon market can resolve global warming at no net cost to the economy. This may seem unbelievable, but it is true. This feature has not been observed until now and needs to be highlighted. Many concerns have been expressed about the costs of averting global warming, which are estimated to be over 1 per cent of the world's gross economic output. This is the basis for opposition to efforts to combat global warming. But these concerns are put to bed by the carbon market in one fell swoop.[1]

Secondly, the carbon market can achieve all this by its own trading operations and requires not a single dollar donation, no taxes and no subsidies, nothing at all. Nada. In fact, it is just the other way around: the carbon market makes money and can stimulate the world economy.

Finally, the carbon market can redress the wealth gap between the rich and the poor nations in a way that benefits both. Yes it can. It has already started increasing productivity and alleviating poverty as nothing else the world has seen until now and can achieve much, much more.[2]

These are bold statements that will not go unchallenged. How does it all work? Read on.

Kyoto, Wealth Creation and Sustainable Development

Kyoto works by the magic of the market. Yes, that is all there is. But do not underestimate what it means and what was achieved. The market is a powerful institution that creates wealth and represents democratic objectives like nothing else. But the market has been badly undermined so far. The 21st century inherited international markets that were ignorant of our physical limits, of the scarcities we now face. This is fair enough because until now human societies were relatively small in a large world, and we could use as much of the planet's atmosphere as we wanted at no cost, for free. But we have reached our limits. We've collided with natural constraints on our use of the atmosphere.

In creating emission caps, the Kyoto Protocol changed all that. Fast. It gave the market the right signal: scarcity is real. We cannot continue to use the atmosphere as a dump – there are limits to that.

After the caps are created, market prices emerge from trading these caps. The carbon market puts a price on emissions; today this is about $30 per tonne. This means that the cost to society of emitting one tonne of carbon is $30. After that, the world markets will not be the same anymore. No longer will we treat the atmosphere as an unlimited resource, a depository for all of the waste that our power plants, vehicles and factories produce. It looks simple and it is simple. It is just a matter of dollars and cents you might think, and what is so great about that?

Not so fast. This is more than dollars and cents. In reality, country-by-country, we have accepted limits on our use of the global atmospheric commons. This is a tremendous feat for it marks a turning point in our relationship to nature. It symbolizes our emerging new consciousness about nature's limits and its vulnerability to human insult and abuse. Perhaps more importantly it signals the start of a new era of global cooperation. If nations can overcome their differences to accept their shared responsibility for the health of the planet and the well-being of future generations, we may be able to find solutions to the other serious crises confronting the global community. In this way, although climate change presents an enormous challenge, by creating the carbon market we have transformed the challenge into an opportunity.

The Kyoto Protocol forges cooperation between rich and poor nations, and unites business and environmental interests, in ways that no other international agreement or market relationship has been able to do thus far. But it is just the beginning. The full potential of the carbon market has yet to be unleashed. In the previous chapter we saw that there are two major obstacles standing in the way: the reluctance of the world's largest greenhouse gas producer, the US, to participate unless countries such as China and India cap their emissions, and the growing hostility toward the CDM by the EU and Japan. Unless we can overcome these obstacles soon Kyoto will expire in 2012 without an alternative to take its place. On all fronts, time is running out. We're running out of time to save Kyoto and we are running out of time to prevent climate change.[3]

The question of whether or not to save Kyoto is not the same as whether or not to combat climate change. Saving Kyoto presumes that all nations agree that there is no greater threat to civilization than climate change. It is priority number one. The question is whether the Kyoto framework is the most appropriate to the task.

If Not Kyoto, What?

The first reaction one hears is that each country could go at it alone. Why not? Why could the US not create its own carbon market, why could it not limit its own emissions? Why do we need international cooperation and cumbersome international agreement? Why not go it alone? Why, indeed?

If a country adopts a go-it-alone approach to emissions reduction, total emissions will not fall sufficiently to avoid the risks of climate change. It is as simple as that. Think of it this way. The US could refrain tomorrow morning from emitting a single tonne of carbon. Yet, emitting nothing itself, the US will still be the victim of climate change and will still suffer the consequences of global warming due to the actions of others. In fact, as we saw in Chapter 1, the OECD estimated in 2008 that a single US city, Miami, in Florida, stands to lose $3.5 trillion in property damages due to climate change. The value of property may decrease with the 2008–2009 financial crisis but the scope of the loss is real. Just one city will suffer trillions in losses due to the actions of other nations. Why does this all happen? Because the US, while the world's largest emitter, still emits only 25 per cent of the world emissions. That is all. The other 75 per cent comes from outside the US territory and is enough, more than enough, to precipitate climate change. Carbon emissions distribute uniformly over the entire planet. It is the ultimate equalizer. Without cooperation we are all doomed together.

Yet if countries cooperate as part of an international treaty, they still need to agree on how to share the burdens of climate mitigation between them. This is exactly what Kyoto starts from: an agreement on limiting greenhouse gas emissions country-by-country. So whether we save Kyoto or not, we need to repeat what the Kyoto Protocol has done, we need to agree on global limits and assign emission limits to the various nations in the world. There is no other way.

Once emission limits are agreed nation-by-nation the carbon market is a natural and desirable way to allow each nation the flexibility to be above its limit one year and below it another year, while still remaining within the global caps. And once you accept that flexibility – hey presto! – you are back to the Kyoto Protocol structure in its full regalia. Kyoto allows each nation to have its own internal control system – carbon taxes, markets, etc. Call it whatever you want but there is no way escaping this simple truth. It is Kyoto or bust.

We Prefer Kyoto – Do You?

It has already been negotiated and it took years to do so. We need to decrease emission limits further and improve the CDM. But what other mechanism has the potential to resolve competing interests as effectively as Kyoto's carbon market?

Can the international community honour the commitment to fairness for developing nations that it made in 1992 at the Earth Summit and still achieve a lower global emissions cap? Is it possible for the international community to have its cake and eat it too – fairness and climate change prevention? Yes, but only because of the unique properties and benefits of a market for a global public good.

We know that Kyoto's carbon market can unite the business interests in rich nations with the clean development needs of poor nations. It has done so already through the CDM, which works alongside the carbon market. The business communities are up in arms to defend the CDM today against the EU Parliament, as are the environmentalists. But to reiterate, the Kyoto Protocol is a market-orientated agreement with three additional properties that make it truly unique and almost impossible to beat:

1)   It creates new wealth to pay for emissions reduction. It can resolve global warming at almost no cost to the economy, thus contradicting the dire warnings that we have heard by many of the world's experts about the costs of averting global warming.

2) It can foster desirable technological change, clean technologies and sustainable economic development across the world. It can support and help fund developing nations' clean industrialization, which is critical for preventing emissions in the future.

3) It can help alleviate poverty in developing nations by transferring wealth from rich to poor nations for clean productive projects, to the benefit of all countries.

The Kyoto Protocol achieves all this using a free market approach, without taxes or regulations, except for the firm limits it places on carbon emissions. This is performance beyond anything we have seen so far. These claims must be carefully argued and explained.

Wealth Creation

The magic of the carbon market is that it pays for itself. Fiscal conservatives should welcome the news that the carbon market is a fully-funded institution. Other than the cost of participating in global climate talks, which establish the rules for international emissions trading, it requires nothing additional of countries' governments.

As we have already discussed, the important thing the global carbon market does is attach a price to carbon emissions. The current price of carbon in the global market is roughly $30 per tonne. The world currently produces the equivalent of 30 gigatonnes of carbon dioxide per year. If we charge emitters $30 for each tonne of carbon they produce, the carbon market can generate $900 billion a year. This is equivalent to 1.5 per cent of global gross domestic product (GDP). This is an enormous new source of wealth that the carbon market creates. We can tap into this wealth to pay for global emissions reduction. In reality, the market will do this all by itself. Whoever can reduce carbon will sell their carbon credit in the carbon market, and will be paid for their work.

In truth the wealth has always existed. It was the planet's wealth – the atmosphere and its capacity to regulate global climate. Before the Kyoto Protocol, emitters effectively claimed the planet's wealth – our common wealth – for their own private use. By pumping carbon and other greenhouse gases into the atmosphere, they drew down our wealth stock. But now, thanks to the carbon market, we have the ability to take back this wealth and reclaim it as our common asset. It is important that we use the global carbon market to distribute this wealth across countries. And we must do it in a way that favours poor nations, that favours us all.

For so many years we have been wrapped up in questions of what it will cost to save the world from climate change and whether we can we afford it, and we over-looked the potential for emissions reduction to pay for itself. As we saw in Chapter 2, the IPCC surveyed the expert literature on climate economics and found that the estimated costs of preventing climate change range from 1 to 3 per cent of global GDP each year. The influential Stern Report to the UK government, by former World Bank Chief Economist Sir Nicholas Stern, estimated that the world would have to spend 1 per cent of global GDP each year to protect against damages as great as 5–20 per cent of global GDP each year in the future. Fortunately the global carbon market will generate $900 billion each year – sufficient revenue to offset the costs of protecting the future against global climate change. The numbers make sense and it is no trick. World GDP is about $65 trillion today. It could cost 1.5 per cent of global GDP, roughly $900 billion each year, to prevent catastrophic climate change. And the carbon market will create a new source of global wealth, $900 billion, which is equivalent to 1.5 per cent of global GDP each year, which will be paid to those who reduce emissions. The net effect on the global economy is zero. Some people will be worse off, and some will be better off. The bad guys, the over-emitters, will pay and the under-emitters will receive their money. But the net effect on the global economy is zero.

Carbon prices should go up in the future, as international trading increases and countries adopt more aggressive timelines for reducing emissions. By some estimates, the carbon market of the

Kyoto Protocol will reach $2 trillion soon, but for as long as the carbon market operates it will facilitate the level of emissions reduction that is required to avert climate change. This presupposes of course that the technologies are there to reduce carbon emissions – the same assumption made in the Stern Report. We have shown how carbon capture and storage including new negative carbon technologies can be used for this purpose. The price of carbon may adjust to reflect the technological reality of what it costs to reduce a tonne of carbon. If the cost for reducing carbon emissions decreases, the market price will go down. This is the magic of the market.

So what does all this mean? It means that using the carbon market to penalize emitters and to require them to pay for emissions will generate enough income to offset the projected costs of preventing climate change. Compared to the commercial reinsurance costs for catastrophic risks discussed in Chapter 2, 1.5 per cent of global GDP to insure the future from climate change seems fair and prudent. The carbon market gives us a way to pay for it. The carbon market guarantees that the emitters will foot the bill. They will pay the premium for all of us. And the market ensures efficient allocation of those dollars to achieve the task.

Still not convinced? Think of it this way: at the global level, the benefits of preserving our climate system must outweigh the costs. According to the Stern Report, the costs of global warming are equivalent to losing 5 to 20 per cent of global GDP now and forever. Though we may not be able to appropriately and accurately measure those benefits, those of us who believe in the science of climate change understand that the benefits of preventing climate change, the lives saved and property damage avoided, are well worth the investment, which, according to the IPCC Assessment Report 4, is about 1 to 3 per cent of global GDP. If preventing climate change generates a global benefit that equals or exceeds the associated global cost, it increases welfare by achieving a more balanced combination between using fossil fuel and environmental quality, which is the aim of the international community, at no extra cost to the global economy.

One must be careful to understand this claim. To say that a successful international effort to avoid climate change can generate a net welfare gain, a global benefit in excess of global cost, is not the same thing as saying that everyone everywhere will be better off because of the carbon market. The carbon market, as we saw, will generate winners and losers. It may hurt some businesses that make large profits generating carbon emissions and some economies that prosper from the export of fossil fuels, while creating new profit opportunities and new development prospects where none previously existed. This is as it should be to create the right incentives for using the planet's atmosphere. No surprises here. But as long as the gains to some sectors and some people offset the losses of others, there will be no net loss to the global economy from our efforts to prevent climate change. That is the magic of the carbon market.

In the US, the political and academic debate over a cap-and-trade programme to reduce US emissions is well underway. The issue is not whether to use a cap-and-trade mechanism but how best to distribute the revenues that the initial sale of carbon permits will generate. The economics literature has shown that it is possible to shield the most economically vulnerable households in the US from the costs of emissions reduction. Recent work demonstrates that if the US distributes the revenues from carbon sales on an equal per capita basis, more than 60 per cent of US households would benefit.[4] The 'dividend' payment that each American would receive would represent her/his claim on a common asset – the US share of the global atmosphere. A cap-and-trade programme in the US has the capacity to generate enough wealth to raise the incomes of almost two-thirds of Americans. This is truly extraordinary.

As we will see, the potential for redistributing wealth exists on a global scale as well. The distribution of emission rights and the CDM are how the world can distribute the benefits of the global carbon market. This is why the distribution should benefit those nations that emit less over and above those that emit more.

But let us again be clear. Even though preventing climate change can make every country better off, there is no guarantee that every country will be better off. The global carbon market creates the right potential and the right incentives but it is still up to us to decide how we distribute the benefits of the carbon market. Imagine that the carbon market is a successful recipe for baking a larger pie for the global community to share. A larger pie means that it is possible for all of us to have a bigger slice. There are many ways for us to divide the larger pie: we can divide the pie in a way that is equitable, giving those countries that have only consumed small slices in the past much larger slices in the present. Or we can divide the pie such that the rich countries' slices get bigger, while other countries' slices shrink or stay the same. Now that we understand why the carbon market should be the recipe for the future, can we agree to divide the pie equitably between us, so that we all benefit? Can we use the carbon market to promote sustainable development and close the global income divide?

Yes, we can. Fostering sustainable development and ending poverty may seem too much to ask for but it is possible and in our view it will happen. This is the magic of Kyoto and its carbon market.

Fostering Sustainable Development

Trading between developed and developing countries can be tricky. Selling one's rights to emit carbon dioxide today means selling one's ability to burn coal and other fossil fuels. Most industrial economies would screech to a halt if they were unable to burn fossil fuels, unless alternative energy sources and technologies were available. By selling their rights to emit, developing countries could be selling their rights to industrialize.

The global carbon market can help solve this dilemma. The richest countries have money but an environmental deficit: they emit 60 per cent of global greenhouse gases even though they make up less than 20 per cent of the world's population. The developing countries are in the opposite situation: they have a credit in the environmental account, but a monetary deficit. They emit less and they house most of the world's remaining forests and biodiversity. There are natural gains from trade between the two groups of countries.

How can the carbon market provide incentives to protect, rather than to destroy, the world's forests? The carbon market gives countries a way to capitalize on the value of their environmental resources. These are the most valuable resources known to humankind. Yet, at present, the only way to realize their value is to destroy them: a forest that preserves biodiversity and contributes to the atmosphere's quality is destroyed to sell the wood of its trees for plank or pulp, or burned to give way to arable land. Carbon markets can help realize the value of environmental assets without destroying them. They can balance out the position of large and small traders by offering a neutral trading base for all. They can provide an anonymous process where several small sellers can meet a few large buyers. Carbon markets can be an important part of restructuring the global financial infrastructure to meet the needs of today's mature industrial economies, as well as those of newly industrializing countries.

Even though the developing nations have no emission caps in the Kyoto Protocol, and therefore cannot trade directly in the carbon market, they can still participate and benefit from the carbon market. This is because of the Clean Development Mechanism, which encourages investment in clean technologies in developing nations and allows developing nations to benefit indirectly from carbon trading. The CDM is the crucial link between emissions reduction and the broader goal of sustainable development. The Kyoto Protocol stipulates that all CDM projects must be able to demonstrate tangible sustainable development benefits for the host country.

We have talked about the CDM before but now we explain how it actually works. When an industrial nation, individual or institution invests in a project inside a developing nation the investor is given a carbon credit based on the amount of carbon that is actually reduced. This carbon credit can then be traded in the carbon market. For example, a project that is proven to reduce carbon emission by one million tonnes will be awarded carbon credits that can be traded in the carbon market at the current carbon price of $30 per tonne. This increases the project's profitability significantly, by decreasing costs by $30 million. This way the CDM produces strong incentives for the development of clean technologies in developing nations and encourages investors in industrial nations to finance such projects. It ensures a flow of investment dollars from North to South, while transferring the technologies of the post-carbon economy to developing nations.

The CDM changes the profit equation in favour of using clean technologies in developing nations. To see this, consider for example two projects in developing countries that are identical in every possible way, except for the technology they use. One project emits 10 million tonnes of carbon, the other project emits no carbon at all. Before the Kyoto Protocol attached a price to carbon emissions, investors had no incentive to choose one technology over the other. But with the CDM, the project using the clean technology, the one that does not produce carbon emissions, becomes $30 million more profitable than the other project.

The CDM is an important and potentially transformative market incentive embedded in the carbon market of the Kyoto Protocol. During the year 2006, the first year in which the carbon

	Annual Average CERs*	Expected CERs until end of 2012**
CDM project pipeline (3000, of which:)	N/A	2,700,000,000
1183 are registered	227,697,552	1,330,000,000
91 are requesting registration	31,237,639	130,000,000

*Assumption: all activities deliver simultaneously their expected annual average emission reductions. **Assumption: no renewal of crediting periods.
Source: UNFCCC.

Distribution of Registered Project Activities by Scope

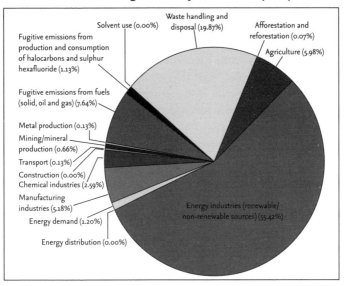

market traded, about $8 billion in such projects were carried out in developing nations. The extension of the Kyoto Protocol carbon market in Europe, the European Emissions Trading Scheme, has already led to transfers of approximately $23 billion since 2006 to poor nations for CDM projects. These projects account for about 20 per cent of the EU's required emissions reduction.[5]

One need only explore the scale and scope of existing project activity under the CDM to understand its transformative potential for the global economy. There are already 1,183 registered CDM projects worldwide, producing more than $227 million Certified Emissions Reduction credits (CERs), 55 per cent of which will be produced in China alone (see table on p148). Each CER is worth one tonne of carbon equivalent emissions. As of 2008, there are over 3,000 CDM projects in the pipeline, at various stages of approval, with the potential to produce 2.7 billion CERs between now and the end of 2012. More than 55 per cent of the projects are aimed at developing renewable energy resources in the host country (see 'Distribution of Registered Project Activities by Scope' on p149).

Each CDM project must qualify through a rigorous public registration and issuance process, the purpose of which is to ensure 'real, measurable and verifiable emissions reductions that are additional to what would have occurred without the project'.[6] The CDM Executive Board, which answers to the nations that have ratified the Kyoto Protocol, oversees the verification and registration of CDM projects.

Clean Development Projects Worldwide[7]

To better understand the real benefits of CDM projects, we describe a handful of current such projects below. These are the official descriptions of the projects and their attendant sustainable development benefits, as reported to the CDM Executive Board for project approval and certification. (See p96 for details on how financial assistance is given and how credits are awarded.)

Inner Mongolia Wind Farm Project
Host Country: China
Associated Country: United Kingdom
The objective of the Inner Mongolia Wind Farm Project is to generate electricity from renewable wind resources. The project will install 33 wind turbines. Total installed capacity will be 49.5MWh. Once the project is put into operation the annual average power delivered to the grid is expected to achieve a level of 115,366MWh and the expected annual emissions reduction is 120,119 tonnes of carbon emission equivalents. Clean and renewable energy will be utilized by the project for the power generation, which is environmentally and socially beneficial. The project will contribute to sustainable development in the following ways:

- Reduction of greenhouse gas emissions and other pollutants.

- Promotion of domestic manufacture and the development of wind power industry in China.
- Increased local revenue and employment opportunities.

Fuel Switching Project of the Aqaba Thermal Power Station
Host Country: Jordan
Associated Country: United Kingdom
The project is to switch from oil to gas at the Aqaba Thermal Power Station (ATPS) in Aqaba, Jordan. ATPS is the largest power plant in Jordan. The fuel switch is from Heavy Fuel Oil (HFO) to Natural Gas (NG), and the capacity of the plant is unchanged as a result of the fuel switch. The project is estimated to reduce an average annual amount of 397,163 tonnes of carbon equivalent emissions over a 10-year crediting period. ATPS initiated this fuel switch because of the plant's negative environmental impacts, which are mostly gaseous and a result of heavy fuel oil combustion for electrical power generation, and because of Jordan's ratification of the Kyoto Protocol and potential CDM benefits, which were considered from the beginning of the project to make it financially viable (despite unfavourable relative fuel prices). The fuel switch will benefit the environment, and contribute to sustainable development as follows:

- Support of the local economy, which is dominated by tourism and therefore benefits greatly from reduced pollution.
- Reduction of shipping/trucking of HFO, with reduction of related traffic and pollution (NG will be imported from Egypt via a submarine pipeline in the Gulf of Aqaba).
- Reduction of greenhouse gas emissions and diversification of Jordan's electricity production with a leaning towards 'cleaner' power.

Biogas Capture and Regeneration at Lekir Palm Oil Mill
Host country: Malaysia
Associated Country: Sweden
The proposed project is to be implemented at Lekir Palm Oil Mill

in Malaysia. The wastewater from the mill is treated through a ponding system. These conditions result in anaerobic conditions within the ponds and biodegradation of the organic content in the wastewater leads to the generation of methane. The proposed project activity is to cover two of the existing open anaerobic open ponds to capture the methane-rich biogas. The treated effluent will then be channeled into the existing subsequent ponds for further polishing. The captured biogas will be combusted in dual fuel generators (fired with a mixture of diesel and biogas) to generate electricity for the project activity while the excess biogas will be flared on site. This process will benefit the environment, and contribute to sustainable development as follows:

- Reduction of the greenhouse gas emissions from the open anaerobic ponds.
- Improvement of air quality through the reduction of odour.
- Creation of job opportunities for the local community during project implementation.
- Enabling the transfer of knowledge and technology on biogas generation, treatment and the utilization of biogas in generators, which should stimulate the development of both the market for generators and the use of biogas as a real alternative energy for the local industries in Malaysia.

Yuexi Dayan Small Hydropower Project
Host Country: China
Associated Country: Sweden

The project is a water-diversion-type run-of-river hydropower project located on the upper reach of the Yangbijiang River in Yunnan Province, China. Electricity generated by the proposed project will displace part of the electricity generated by South China Power Grid, which is dominated by coal-fired power plants, and thus greenhouse gas emission reductions will be achieved. The average annual emission reductions of the proposed project are estimated to be 97,403 tonnes of carbon emission equivalents. The proposed project will promote local sustainable development by making use of renewable hydropower. Major contributions of the proposed project are as follows:

- The proposed project will be the major power plant in Yangbi Yi Autonomous County and will play an important role in developing local resources such as silicon, antimony and molybdenum, which can help local poverty reduction.
- Alleviation of the shortage of electricity and improvement of the power quality of the grid to ensure smooth industrial and agricultural production and meet the need for electricity in the daily life of the ethnic minorities in the region.
- Reduction of the emission of pollutants and greenhouse gases that might otherwise be caused by coal-fired generators so as to improve local environment.
- Creation of local jobs.
- After the operation of the proposed project, the local people can substitute firewood with electricity, which will reduce the damage to the local vegetation and protect the local ecology.

Facilitating Reforestation for Guangxi Watershed Management in Pearl River Basin

Host Country: China
Associated Countries: Italy, Spain
The proposed project aims to explore and demonstrate the technical and methodological approaches related to credible carbon sequestration (CCS) and pilot the viability of enhancing the livelihoods of people and the natural environment by facilitating reforestation activities in watershed areas along the Pearl River Basin. The project will generate the income to the poor farmers/communities by enabling the carbon sequestered by plantations to act as a virtual cash crop for the local project beneficiaries who will gain direct benefits from harvesting the

plantation as well as from the sale of carbon credits, which will in turn reduce the threats to natural forests. In addition, forest restoration in this area plays a vital role in biodiversity conservation, soil and water conservation and poverty alleviation, while sequestering carbon dioxide from the atmosphere. The sustainable development potential of the project is as follows:

- Sequestering of carbon through forest restoration in small watershed areas and testing and piloting how reforestation activities generate high-quality emission reductions in greenhouse gases that can be measured, monitored and verified.
- Enhancement of biodiversity conservation by increasing the connectivity of forests adjacent to nature reserves.
- Improvement of soil and water erosion control.
- Generation of income for local communities.

Agricultural Waste Management System Emissions Mitigation
Host Country: Mexico
Associated Countries: Switzerland, United Kingdom
This project proposes to apply to confined animal (swine) feeding operations in central Mexico, a greenhouse gas mitigation methodology that is applicable to intensive livestock operations. The proposed project activities will mitigate greenhouse gas emissions in an economically sustainable manner, and will result in other environmental benefits, such as improved water quality and reduced odour. In simple terms, the project proposes to move from a high-emissions animal waste management system – an open air lagoon – to a lower-emissions animal waste management practice – an ambient temperature anaerobic digester with capture and combustion of resulting biogas. The purpose of this project is to mitigate animal effluent-related greenhouse gas emissions by improving animal waste management systems. It has the potential to reduce approximately 4.3 million tonnes of carbon emission equivalents each year. Its contribution to sustainable development is as follows:

- Protection of human health and the environment through proper handling of large quantities of animal waste.
- Methane recovery project activity will upgrade livestock operations infrastructure and will enable the use of renewable energy sources.
- Improvement of air quality (reduction of the emission of Volatile Organic Compounds and odour).
- Incentive for future farm projects that will have an additional positive impact on greenhouse gas emissions with an attendant potential for reducing groundwater contamination problems.
- Increased local employment of skilled labourers for the fabrication, installation, operation and maintenance of the specialized equipment.
- Establishment of a model for world-class, scalable animal waste management practices, which can be duplicated on other livestock farms throughout Mexico, dramatically reducing livestock related greenhouse gas emissions and providing the potential for a new source of revenue and green power.

Kuyasa Low-Cost Urban Housing Energy Upgrade, Cape Town
Host Country: South Africa
Associated Country: none
This project is aimed as an intervention in an existing low-income housing development with households in Kuyasa, as well as in future housing developments in this area. The project aims to improve the thermal performance of the existing and future housing units, improve lighting and water heating efficiency. This will result in reduced current and future electricity consumption per household and significant avoided carbon emissions per unit. Other benefits of the project activity include a reduction in local air pollution with subsequent decreases in pulmonary pneumonia, carbon monoxide poisoning and other respiratory illnesses. A decrease in accidents and

damage to property as a result of fire is also anticipated. The project activity relates to the following three interventions per household unit: i) insulated ceilings; ii) solar water heater installation; and iii) energy efficient lighting. It contributes to sustainable development as follows:

- Improved end-use energy efficiency combined with the use of solar energy for water heating will result in measurable avoided pollutant emissions and measurable energy consumption savings. This contributes to 'energy poverty' alleviation.
- By increasing the use of renewable energy and improving thermal performance, cleaner energy services are provided with respect to local pollutants, and cheaper than in the baseline situation. The improvements in the thermal performance will moderate indoor air temperature with associated comfort and health benefits.

Substituting Biofuels and Municipal Solid Waste in Cement Manufacturing, Tamil Nadu
Host Country: India
Associated Country: Germany
The project activity is the partial replacement of fossil fuels with alternate fuels (de-oiled rice bran, municipal solid waste, tyre) in cement manufacturing at Grasim Industries Limited-Cement Division South, Tamil Nadu, India. The purpose is to reduce carbon emissions in cement production by using alternative fuels. Conventionally fossil fuels, namely coal, lignite and pet coke are used in the kiln system for clinker formation. The project involves partial replacement of the fossil fuels with alternative fuels, such as agricultural by-products, tyres and municipal solid waste (in the form of refuse-derived fuel), all of which are lower greenhouse gas-emitting fuels. This will result in significant saving on non-renewable fossil fuel as the project has the potential to mitigate 51,932 metric tonnes of carbon emissions equivalent per annum. Utilization of these alternative fuels would require retrofitting of the existing facility and

installation of fuel processing equipments. This type of project is not common because it is not normally financially viable without CDM financing. Its sustainable development potential is as follows:

- Substitution of lower-emission fuels for fossil fuels.
- More effective disposal of waste by using it as an alternative fuel.
- Generation of employment opportunities in agricultural-by-product supply chain.
- Generation of employment for skilled and unskilled workers of the rural region.
- Creation of an additional source of revenue for farmers' agricultural by-products, which were earlier burnt in open grounds and fetched no value.

Closing the Global Divide

The climate crisis is a classic example of over-exploitation of a common property resource, often called 'the tragedy of the commons'. The atmosphere is a resource that all people on the planet share. Throughout history we have polluted this resource without consideration for how it diminishes our use of the resource or how it diminishes the use of the resource for the billions of other people we share it with. We never had an incentive to economize on our use of the atmosphere, because there was never any cost for using it. The atmosphere belonged to all of us and to none of us at the same time.

With this simplistic, yet accurate, depiction of the problem, the logic of the Kyoto Protocol becomes clearer. Since no country was empowered to restrict access to the atmosphere, and no country had an incentive to limit its own use, the only chance we had of preserving the atmosphere for ourselves and for future generations was to collectively agree to a cap on global emissions. By capping global emissions, the Kyoto Protocol transformed something that we had historically treated as unlimited in supply – the atmosphere's capacity to absorb greenhouse gas emissions – into something that was finite. It created scarcity where none had previously been acknowledged. That scarcity now imposes a cost on our use of the atmospheric commons. For the first time in history, we pay a price for polluting the atmosphere.

What the Kyoto Protocol essentially did was create property rights – user rights – to a shared resource. We can think of these user rights as emissions rights; the right to emit a fixed quantity of carbon dioxide into the atmosphere. But limiting access to the atmosphere was only step one. The more difficult task for Kyoto was to allocate those user rights to nations. It did this by assigning emission limits to countries. The limits specified the percentage reduction in emissions that each country had to achieve by the end of the first commitment period. Implicit in each country's emissions limit was its share of global emissions rights. The lower a country's emissions limit, the fewer user rights it was granted, and the more it was required to cut its emissions.

To fully understand the conflicts threatening the future of the Kyoto Protocol, it is important to recognize that the allocation of emissions rights is a form of wealth transfer between nations. The absence of emissions caps on developing countries' emissions essentially means that they have unlimited access to the atmospheric commons. In this sense, the Kyoto Protocol capped only the largest portion of global emissions, the portion coming from industrialized countries. By granting developing countries unlimited user rights to the atmosphere, the Kyoto Protocol allowed, through the CDM, a huge incentive for clean productive investments in poor nations, one that is virtually unrivaled in international affairs. Emissions rights are highly valuable commodities, especially when those rights can be traded in a global carbon market. The allocation of emission rights is a potent tool for increasing clean productive investment between nations and we can use it in a deliberate way to close the global income divide and prevent global warming.

There is a somewhat surprising feature of the carbon market that militates in favour of equity. Unlike all other markets, the carbon market protects poor countries as a condition of market efficiency, therefore in the carbon market efficiency demands fairness. There is no other market for which this is true. In all other markets, outcomes can be efficient but highly unfair at the same time; this is the reason why people can mistrust markets. That cynicism need not be carried over to the carbon market.

The 'commodity' that carbon markets trade is, in reality, different from any other commodity ever traded: it is a global public good. As a result there is an important link between each nation's right to emit and the efficiency of the market. This has important implications for market behaviour.[8] Because carbon dioxide is distributed so uniformly and stably around the planet, the resulting concentration of carbon dioxide is the same for everyone around the world. This concentration cannot be chosen independently by each trader – we all face the same concentration of carbon dioxide. This uniformity is one way of characterizing a global public good. Classic public goods are those whose supply is the same for everyone involved, for example the armed forces, bridges and school systems. Markets that trade the rights to use public goods are different from standard markets for private goods, such as corn, machines, houses, stocks and bonds. In standard markets traders decide how much of different goods to consume, and they do so independently from each other. Each trader identifies their optimal level of consumption of a good based on their preferences and what they can afford. What the optimal level of consumption is for one trader is not necessarily the optimal level of consumption for another.

The Kyoto Protocol specifies the same carbon dioxide concentration in the atmosphere for all countries. Given the stark differences in countries' incomes and what they can afford the concentration that the Kyoto Protocol specifies is not necessarily optimal for all countries. Indeed, it is most likely beyond what most developing nations can afford. Developing countries use little energy and produce few emissions compared with the rest of the world. They confront more immediate short-term demands to satisfy basic needs, such as those to feed, clothe and educate their populations.

For these reasons, it is inefficient to require developing countries to purchase more global emissions abatement than they can afford at this point in time. But this is exactly what the carbon market of the Kyoto Protocol does – what it has to do since emissions abatement is a global public good and we all share the same atmosphere.

The only way to solve the problem, to make it efficient or optimal for developing countries to purchase Kyoto's level of global emissions reduction, is to increase clean investment in developing countries and allow them to reduce emissions to reach the levels agreed for the world as a whole. We could do this directly, through lump sum payments to developing countries along the lines of what international aid agencies try to do. We could also issue 'side payments' to induce developing countries to accept emissions caps.[9] But the magnitude of the wealth transfers that would be required in these cases is far greater than any income transfer we have seen before. You can imagine the uproar in rich nations if governments began transferring huge sums of wealth directly to nations such as India or China.

The magic of the carbon market is that it avoids these issues. Remember that the carbon market creates a new source of global wealth. It can use this wealth to close the income divide between rich and poor countries, something that no other international trading agreement has ever been able to do. By giving developing countries more rights to use the global atmosphere than rich countries, and allowing developing countries to sell those rights, the carbon market transfers wealth from North to South, but only when the CDM applies and they reduce global carbon emissions. It is fair but also productive and efficient. The Kyoto Protocol already provides more rights to emit to poor nations than richer ones – but it is not without controversy.

Preserving this most unique and magical feature of Kyoto is perhaps the greatest challenge confronting us. Will we turn our back on Kyoto's potential? The potential to unite countries, close the global income divide, and save us from climate change? Will the global community save Kyoto?

Financial Turmoil: What Kyoto Means to the Future | 7

In a world in turmoil, Kyoto is more at risk than ever. For most people the state of economic turmoil throws up a whole new question mark over climate change policy. Taking action was already an uphill struggle and the state of the world economy has made the hill even steeper. Even before the recent economic turmoil there had been growing concerns in Europe about the costs of controlling energy use as a means of keeping the lid on greenhouse gas emissions. Europe and Japan have been the most steadfast supporters of climate change policy but now Europe is witness to division in the debate over next steps to achieve its emission goals, while the Kyoto Clean Development Mechanism (CDM) is being challenged in the European Parliament.[1]

On the other side of the Atlantic, there is eager anticipation of President Barack Obama offering a dramatically different policy on climate change. Yet this hope is also tempered by the chill winds of the financial crisis. Environmental groups are already bracing themselves for delays or disappointment on action to tackle global warming which, many say, will inevitably be seen as having an impact on American jobs.

Together with the potentially catastrophic risks we face, this book has also illuminated unique opportunities that countries face as a consequence of global climate change. It has revealed the potential of Kyoto's carbon market to unite business and environmental interests, forge cooperation between rich and poor nations, induce much-needed investment in green development, and close the global wealth divide. Put like this, the future looks promising.

We have arrived at the point of no return. This is where the new path begins, one in which the promising changes we describe can occur. Business and environmentalist interests can converge, the carbon market can provide the incentives needed for new technologies and can help pay the cost of averting climate change and the CDM will help to even up the score between the super rich nations and those who are in the midst of abject poverty. But it is a race against time.

The financial turmoil in the global economy is working against us. It has destroyed faith in markets (and many would say that it is the wrong time to reinvent markets) but in all fairness, this is not new. It is a recurrent theme in capitalistic society. Capitalism is all about taking risks. The entire system is built on the corporation, a unique type of animal that is idiosyncratic to capitalism. The corporation is nothing but a risk-taking machine, an incentive to take economic risks. The distinguishing feature of the corporation is that it caps the losses that it may incur on the downside. This is specific to corporations and is called 'limited liability'. Through bankruptcy laws the corporation can wipe the slate clean, taking much of the sting out of economic failure and moving to a better future. It is no wonder capitalist societies are innovative, creative and at the same time intrinsically risky. They are built to be this way. And it is no wonder that every so often they get into serious trouble. This is what risk means. It means that most of the time things go well or even very well, but sometimes things go wrong, very wrong, badly wrong. So why should we be surprised when they do?

The reason is that the world today is so interconnected that the economic shocks from excesses are transmitted through the world economy with lightening speed and the shockwaves leave no stone unturned.[2] We are facing a new economic stage, where the connection between financial institutions the world over is so extreme that any single default can lead to widespread defaults and financial failure.[3]

This is exactly what is happening today in the aftershock of the property market downturn in the US and elsewhere. Defaults on house mortgages that are twice historical standards, 9.15 per cent rather than 4.3 per cent in the US, are creating deep losses in mortgage-based securities that were made by bundling millions of mortgages together. This allowed uncovered positions with huge leverages by the large financial institutions that traded credit default swaps and options over and above mortgage-backed securities, markets that involve over $530 trillion in trades; almost ten times the entire economic product of the planet.[4]

Yet as difficult as the situation is today, the main problems we face are not caused by the excesses and follies of capitalism, which bring us many gains as well as shocking damages in its wake. All this is all heartbreaking and destructive but it is also relatively reversible. It is cyclical; the economic down cycle will take its course, and will eventually revert itself.

Investing in a Time of Economic Uncertainty

The larger problem we face now is created by irreversible changes that we are unleashing on the metabolism of the planet itself. For the first time in recorded history, humans are changing the planet in ways that endanger its basic life support systems. This is real. It could be reversed in geological time, but it is irreversible in a timescale that matters for us humans.

With every challenge comes opportunity. The Kyoto Protocol, the first international agreement based on the creation of a new international market for a global public good, shows the way. If we can save the Kyoto Protocol, we could prevent irreversible losses. There are two rays of hope to save Kyoto, new technologies and new market mechanisms that can unite industrial and developing nations.

As far as the new technologies are concerned there is a short-term strategy and a long-term strategy, and the one naturally blends into the other. In the short term, carbon capture technologies can relatively quickly capture and safely store away the carbon in the atmosphere, so as to avert climate change. This could be achieved in the next 20 years, using the negative carbon technologies discussed above. And this strategy can mesh with a long-term target of turning away from fossil fuel addiction and towards renewable and carbon-free energy sources such as wind, solar, hydroelectric energy, thermal energy and even nuclear energy.

But in the short term we have a lot to worry about. The Kyoto protocol, our only tool for global action, our only international agreement on the carbon issue, is itself at risk.

It is possible to resolve the problem of climate change. The carbon market, with its innate market magic, can help achieve a solution at no net cost to society as we have already seen. But first we need to save Kyoto. We must sort out the immediate political issue that divides the US and the rest of the world between now and December 2009, when the nations of the world are supposed to vote, in Copenhagen, for the global climate regime that will prevail after 2012.

The immediate political issue we need to resolve is the demand on the part of the US to cap Chinese and developing nations' emissions before it will ratify the Protocol and live to its signed promises to reduce emissions. We know that China and the other developing nations (G77) oppose any limits today, when they are still poor nations, and their position is supported by Article 4 of the 1992 Climate Convention. However, we have already seen how this last bump of the road can be overcome: by adopting new financial strategies based on the carbon market but going well beyond it, which effectively give each side what they want.

In order to forecast a realistic future for Kyoto, we need to provide a realistic assessment of the two solutions proposed: the political solution to overcome the issue of developing nations' caps, and the technological solution that involves capturing carbon. This is a tall order, but it seems necessary. And just to raise the bar higher, we need to ask ourselves how one may apply the same Kyoto magic to other global environmental problems such as biodiversity and ecosystem destruction. This is not just to raise the bar higher; it is also a practical issue. For without finding a practical solution to the problem of ecosystem destruction and biodiversity extinction, there may be no human species and no carbon emissions to worry about in the first place. We are, after all, in the midst of the largest extinction in the planet, according to scientists, only comparable with the disappearance of the dinosaurs 60 million years ago. Humans would not have survived that period of extinction anymore than the mighty dinosaurs did and it is a serious question whether we can survive this one. We need to understand how a Kyoto-like template can deal with the other global environmental challenges of our time.

Let us focus first on the challenges involved in the technology for carbon capture. Nobuo Tanaka, Executive Director of the IEA, recently reviewed the status of the technology for capturing and storing the gas which, he said, 'must play a key role, but first they must be proven in the next decade.' In 2009, Canada and the US started negotiating a North American environmental and energy accord, to ensure energy supply while fighting greenhouse emissions. The Canadian government has provided $375 million to help develop CCS technology in recent years, and has set up a five-year, $1-billion green technology fund. President Obama specifically referred to CCS as a way to reduce emissions without crippling the economy; the 2009 US economic stimulus package increased federal support by 70 per cent to $8 billion for demonstrations and deployment; new initiatives exist in Illinois, Texas, Pennsylvania, North Dakota and Kansas.

The IEA has published a new blueprint for expanding carbon dioxide capture and storage.[5] The report, while saying the technology is vital if the concentration of the greenhouse gas is ever to be stabilized later this century, warns that the world's countries are not pursuing large-scale tests at anywhere near the required pace and size. The agency notes that the group of eight industrialized powers (G8) agreed earlier this year that 20 large-scale gas-capturing projects should be committed to by 2010. But, the report says, 'Current spending and activity levels are nowhere near enough to achieve these deployment goals.'

All of this tends to circle back around to the idea that the most effective path forward on climate today is direct investment in research, development and demonstration plants of non-polluting energy technologies, and even more to the point, negative carbon technologies as described earlier in the book.[6] Many climate campaigners and politicians have put two issues at the forefront of their climate agendas: first, passing legislation capping carbon dioxide emissions without which no action will ever be taken; and second demonstrating technology for capturing and burying the main human-generated greenhouse gas. This process is often called 'clean coal' technology, but it goes further and is different from established methods for scrubbing directly harmful pollution, such as sulfur dioxide, from emissions. Turning these plans into action has been complicated by recent ballooning deficits. Yet unless we take action fast it is a technology that will remain a pipe dream. We need to take immediate action to demonstrate the carbon capture technologies – ideally negative carbon technologies – work as soon as possible.

The first order of the day has to be to reaffirm and lower global carbon caps. This means to reaffirm Kyoto's goals for the post 2012 period. The second order of the day is to create demonstration plants for carbon capture and storage in negative carbon technologies. Negative carbon technologies capture more carbon than they emit. Clean coal is only carbon neutral and does not help nearly as much – it simply continues the status quo on existing emissions – which means 30 gigatonnes per year. The second order of the day can help the first: if the nations voting in Copenhagen realize that technologies exist to make the post 2012 regime possible, feasible and economically reasonable, it is much more likely that they will vote to continue Kyoto after 2012. And to help resolve the US and China impasse, and more generally the impasse between rich and the poor nations, the third order is to adopt a new global financial mechanism based on the carbon market that effectively gives each of the two sides what they want, truly a two-sided coin. This is the solution for the Bali Roadmap, in a nutshell.

Is Kyoto the Solution to Other Environmental Problems?

What about the future of the global environment as a whole? Can Kyoto offer a template to help other fundamental environmental problems of our times, beyond global warming? The short answer is yes, but it requires a bit more explanation as to the why and how.

Why should we worry about the global environment? Because human civilization could not have arrived at this point of flirting with disaster, of irrevocably damaging our planet's climate system, without endangering other natural systems as well. The atmosphere's capacity to absorb and to recycle human waste is not the only ecological limit that we have broached. Indeed, this is the reality of the 21st century: every natural system worldwide is in a state of serious decline. If the 20th century is considered the century of technological innovation and knowledge advancement, the 21st century will be considered the century of reckoning – of reconciling our knowledge and capabilities with the earth's delicate balance and our wealth and power with the basic needs of the earth's majority.

From our forests to our fisheries, our atmosphere to our soil, our watersheds to our farmlands, decades of human exploitation and misuse have reached epidemic proportions. We are witnessing a rate of species loss worldwide that is one thousand times greater than any previous extinction on earth – including the sudden and massive die-off of the dinosaurs.[7] Over six billion people share a planet that is increasingly diminished in its capacity to support life. We cannot afford to deny this reality. How much longer will the earth be able to sustain us?

Kyoto and the Wealth of Nations

Unless we can arrest the deterioration of ecosystem services worldwide, human well-being and prosperity will undoubtedly decline. The links are clear and well-understood. Biodiversity loss undermines the basic needs of human societies. For many of us, it seems clear that we have arrived at a crucial crossroads in history.

Water is a critical example. The biodiversity in watersheds (ecosystems that encompass our water resources) provides fresh water supplies for drinking and irrigation, erosion control and purification. These services are essential to human survival. Poorly managed watersheds are unable to provide water filtration or erosion control, which is essential for water catchment and regulating flood waters. Consequently, we now face a global water crisis with profound implications for global food security, human health and aquatic ecosystems. Population growth, rising standards of living, irrigation for agriculture and industrial production are pushing freshwater demands to unprecedented levels, while mismanagement, pollution and climate change threaten existing freshwater supplies. By 2025, one-third of all people on the planet will face severe and chronic water shortages. Like climate change, the worst ramifications of the global water crisis will be felt by the world's poorest inhabitants.[8]

The climate crisis is the epitome of the global ecological crisis and the future of the planet and of humankind is at stake. The health and vitality of ecosystems, basic human needs and equity are intertwined. But from this common ground we can build anew. The strategy for the future is not only to replace what has been lost – if that is even possible – but to invest in what still remains. The lesson we have learned is that we cannot easily and cheaply replicate ecosystem services with human-engineered substitutes. For example, human-built water filtration systems require billions of dollars to replace the natural filtration services that biodiversity provides at no cost. Viewed in this light, the degradation of watersheds makes little economic sense, whereas investing in watershed restoration and protection does.[9]

In 1996, the city of New York confronted two options for bringing its water supply in line with Environmental Protection Agency (EPA) regulations: it could invest in natural capital or physical capital. Which did it choose? New York City's water comes from a watershed in the Catskill Mountains. The Catskill watershed was so degraded by fertilizers, pesticides and sewage that it could not longer filter and purify the city's drinking water to EPA standards. Investing in natural capital meant buying critical lands in the watershed, restoring and protecting these lands and subsidizing the construction of better sewage treatment facilities. The total cost for restoring the watershed was estimated to cost between $1–1.5 billion.[10] What about the alternative?[11]

The alternative was to build a filtration plant with sufficient capacity to clean New York City's water supply. The estimated cost for this capital project was $6–$8 billion. The choice in this case was straightforward – by investing $1.5 billion in natural capital, the City saved $8 billion in physical capital costs. But the bottom line was even better than these estimates led city planners to believe. By restoring the watershed, the City helped to protect other important ecosystem services, such as biodiversity and carbon sequestration.[12]

We face similar choices with respect to our forest resources. Plantation forests can stabilize soil loss and sequester carbon, but they can't substitute for the diversity and vitality of natural forest ecosystems. Yet forests are disappearing worldwide at a phenomenal pace. We lose 7.3 million hectares of forests each year, an area the size of Panama or Sierra Leone.[13] At present, the only way to realize the value of our forests is to destroy them, to sell the wood for pulp or to burn it to give way to arable land. The attendant ecosystem destruction undermines the health needs of populations around the world, in rich and poor countries alike.

Environmental degradation worldwide results in a loss of ecosystem services valued at $2–$5 trillion each year.[14] This is the startling result of a recent study of the G8's Potsdam Initiative for Biological Diversity. Losses of this magnitude are astounding. We lose more in natural capital each year than what Wall Street lost, $1–1.5 trillion, during the meltdown of financial markets in the autumn of 2008.[15] And it is natural capital, not financial capital, which ultimately determines human wellbeing.

The air we breathe, the water we drink, the soil we grow our food from, the fuel that powers our production, the traditional knowledge that informs our medical techniques, the species that enrich our psychic and emotional health and the amenities we rely on for recreation and our enjoyment of natural beauty, these are what comprise the planet's natural capital stock. And this stock of wealth faces much graver dangers than the runaway lending, greed and plummeting home values that threatened the global financial system. Once this wealth is gone, it cannot be recreated. Therefore we must innovate new ways of protecting it.

There is an enormous disconnection worldwide between the value that biodiversity provides to humans, which derives from satisfying basic human needs for water, food and medicines, and the economic value that can be realized from biodiversity in terms of dollars and cents. The ecosystem services we depend on are almost all examples of public goods. Like the atmosphere, we can trace the degradation of these critical ecosystem services to the absence of prices and clear rules of ownership. These are resources that all people on the planet share or have access to. We have used them and abused them throughout history, with little consideration for how our use diminishes the value of these resources for others or for future generations. We have never had the right incentives to conserve these resources because there was never the right price tag attached to their use. As a result, we may now pay the ultimate price.

Biological diversity, the planet's store of wealth and of knowledge, belongs to all of us and to none of us at the same time. It belongs to the future. That future depends on investing in the natural capital that is abundant on the planet and harnessing its potential for the betterment of all. We need to find ways to capitalize on the value of environmental assets without destroying them. But we must do it in a way that preserves the rights of everyone to fair and sustainable use. The earth and all of its natural riches cannot be sold to the highest bidder. Instead, we can sell shares in the returns from natural capital, while maintaining our collective claims to those natural assets.

The Solution?

In the appropriate context, ecotourism is an excellent case-in-point. Ecotourism has emerged as the primary source of foreign exchange earnings for countries such as Costa Rica, Guatemala and Thailand. Foreigners from wealthier but environmentally poorer areas pay to experience the rare biodiversity within destination countries. These countries are, in essence, selling access to their resources but the underlying assets, the forests and the biological diversity, are not for sale. Ecotourism allows the host country to generate a stream of much needed revenue from its stock of natural wealth. In so doing, it provides an incentive to conserve and protect ecosystem wealth rather than to liquidate it in order to sell the attendant forest products and agricultural commodities in international markets.

Within limits, ecotourism is a service that some developing countries are uniquely positioned to sell because of their abundance of natural resources. In this sense, it is potentially an equalizing force between rich and poor. The primary concerns with ecotourism, however, are the cultural and social impacts that it can produce and how the dividends from that wealth are distributed within the host country. It is critical that the host country distributes the revenues from ecotourism fairly; otherwise its citizens will be denied their share of the benefits from preserving their natural habitats and they will lack incentives to protect it. These are crucial issues that will ultimately determine the long-term success of ecotourism or any global environmental market in promoting conservation. Much of this depends, however, on a country's own internal wealth and income distribution and cannot be solved at the international level. It is important to note that the same is true for climate change or any other global environmental issue. The Kyoto Protocol can distribute the burden of emissions reduction fairly between countries but individual countries are the only ones empowered to decide how to distribute the costs and benefits across their own populations.

Most of the developing nations of the world contain an abundance of natural resources: forests, minerals, fossil fuels, fisheries and the attendant biodiversity. With so much wealth, how is it that these countries struggle to satisfy basic needs? It is because the global economy, as currently structured, has no mechanisms for recognizing and rewarding natural wealth. The only way for countries to capitalize on this wealth is to destroy it. For most developing nations, this means selling resources in international commodity markets, with little additional value added. For example, selling raw wood, not furniture, coffee beans, not coffee. This ensures that developing countries are paid as little as possible for the goods they export, while paying top dollar for the finished goods and services they import. Reliance on natural resources for export condemns developing nations to poverty, while destroying the planet's rich biodiversity. There is a name for this phenomenon: the natural resource curse. It plagues some of the most biologically rich and diverse countries in the world. Can we turn this curse into fortune?

Markets for global public goods, which have unique properties that link equity and efficiency in ways that stand them apart from all other markets, may help solve this dilemma. The world is waking up to the need to protect our remaining natural capital. Much of the demand for environmental protection comes from rich countries, where centuries of industrialization have left them with a debit in their environmental account. The developing countries are in the opposite situation: they have a credit in the environmental account but a financial deficit. They have produced less and they house most of the world's remaining forests and biodiversity. There are natural gains from trade between the two groups of countries.

Global biodiversity, like emissions abatement, is a global public good. Once biodiversity is protected, all countries will benefit from it, albeit to different extents. Countries can't choose different levels of global biodiversity based on their incomes and preferences. This is what makes a market for global public goods different from all other markets. To bring each country's demand – its purchasing power – in line with the level of biodiversity protection that the global community has set as its goal, we will have to shift wealth from rich to poor countries. To do so is not only fair, but it is a condition for market efficiency in markets for global public goods.

Right now, we need developing countries to achieve a higher level of biodiversity conservation than what they might otherwise choose, given their pressing development needs. This is similar to how the Kyoto Protocol asks developing countries to sign up to a higher level of global emissions reduction than they can presently afford. Just as it made sense and it was efficient for the Kyoto Protocol to allocate emissions rights to the benefit of developing countries, so it is fair and efficient to have payments for ecosystem services flow to developing nations.

Markets for global public goods facilitate payments for ecosystem services. Markets for global public goods cannot emulate, in theory or in practice, any other markets that have existed thus far. Because they trade in a good that is universally consumed, the stability of the atmosphere and biological diversity, efficiency demands that the market works to the benefit of poor nations. Done right, payments for ecosystem services can be an equalizing force between nations; a way of levelling the playing field between rich and poor in an era of growing environmental awareness and dire resource needs.

To create these markets, however, we have to decide who owns this natural wealth. Markets cannot trade in goods and services whose ownership is not clearly defined. We need to define this wealth as common wealth, and distribute user rights to the countries who need them most. This is what the Kyoto Protocol achieved with respect to the atmosphere. It created user rights to the global atmospheric commons and distributed those user rights to the benefit of developing nations.

Before the Kyoto Protocol, emitters effectively claimed the planet's wealth, our common wealth, for free and for their own private use. By emitting greenhouse gases into the atmosphere, they diminished the atmosphere's climate regulating capacity. In a similar way, the international oil companies, the multinational logging interests, the bio-prospecting pharmaceutical companies, the agricultural behemoths and even rich nations themselves, have pillaged the natural wealth stock of the planet for decades. The time is right to reclaim this wealth as our common asset and to share the dividends equitably between us.

The Kyoto Protocol Shows The Way

Payments for ecosystem services could in principle provide incentives for preserving, and investing in, the planet's natural wealth and are similar to the voluntary carbon markets that were created in the US, for example the Chicago Climate Exchange (see p101). To achieve this goal in a sustainable fashion:

- They must promote the conservation of biological diversity.
- They must encourage sustainable use, equitable access and benefit sharing of biological resources across the world.
- The payments should be financially self-sustaining and incorporate local communities, governments and the private sector.
- The payments should address the basic needs of developing countries, especially the poor, women, indigenous and local communities.

These principles combined make for a tall order. Are payments for ecosystem services up to the task? While they have achieved some successes, it is generally recognized that without a proper market structure including assigning property rights, payments for ecosystem services and other voluntary markets do not have a future. No other financial mechanism or market is subject to such demanding conditions, except for the Kyoto Protocol carbon market, which satisfies them all. Then again, no other market mechanism trades as directly in the wealth of the planet.

The carbon market is the most developed form of payment for an ecosystem service operating at the international level. Through Kyoto's CDM, projects in developing countries that deliver legitimate and certifiable carbon offsets receive payments from carbon emitters in developed countries. The bad guys pay the good guys; the rich countries pay the poor. The market is fair but because of the unique properties of global public goods, it is also efficient.

The Kyoto Protocol, and its experience with innovative and positive incentives for combating climate change, provides inspiration for addressing other global environmental issues. It supplies a model for combining equity and efficiency in the protection of the earth's endangered biodiversity. Thus there is more at stake in saving the Kyoto Protocol than solely preventing climate change.

We have shown that the Kyoto Protocol's innovative carbon market is an example of the principles of payments for ecosystem services in practice. Kyoto's carbon market provides:

- A carbon price signal that rewards carbon reducers and penalizes excessive emitters, thus helping to avert global warming.
- A means to fund emissions reduction without donation or the need to create global taxing authorities. It is self funded.
- A means to transfer wealth from rich to poor nations in the form of productive and clean investment through the CDM.

Can we emulate the potential of the Kyoto Protocol in other areas where the ecological crises now manifests? Yes, but only if we can save the Kyoto Protocol. If the global community can solve the climate crisis, the most significant challenge civilization has ever faced, we can solve other global environmental problems such as water scarcity and biodiversity destruction. Everything is possible.

Final Thoughts

For the first time in human history, the future of the planet hangs in the balance. Developing nations are in a position to tip that balance one way or the other. Developing nations are home to the majority of the world's population, forests, biodiversity, languages, cultures and indigenous knowledge. The future depends on whether we can preserve these precious resources and overcome the global divide.[16] We know that business-as-usual is a recipe for their destruction. If developing nations pursue the same development path that rich nations set out on two centuries ago, the world will be a far more diminished place as a result. Rich countries blazed a path that was as ruinous as it was profitable. The path led to phenomenal wealth and prosperity for a minority of the world's citizens and ecological destruction for the planet. How can we close that path to the majority, without preventing access to prosperity? Are there other pathways to the future?

What an enormous dilemma we have created. Conflict between rich and poor countries over access to resources defined the new geopolitics in the 21st century. How will this play out? Rich countries can try and use their power and wealth to control the world's endangered resources, or they can work cooperatively with developing countries to chart a cleaner development course. Rich countries can try to preserve their current lifestyles while condemning the developing world to poverty, or they can reduce their own demands on the biosphere to allow room for developing countries to grow. The defining conflicts in the 21st century will be over access to the world's remaining resources. The industrialized world may try to seize control of those resources, just as it may try to impose emissions caps on developing nations but it may not be successful.

So much of the US's antagonism toward the Kyoto Protocol can be understood in this context. The US is not yet willing to concede the need to alter its own course, yet it understands the dire implications if other countries emulate its growth. The US still finds it easier to point a finger at China and its growing energy needs, or India with its many mouths to feed, than to confront its own resource addiction. Like every addict who passes through stages of denial on the way to recovery, we must eventually realize that the fundamental problem and solution lies within. But will this epiphany come too late to save us all from climate disaster?

No matter how hard rich nations may try to sustain their current trajectories, it simply won't work. Even if rich countries denied the entire developing world access to the atmosphere, the emissions from the industrialized world's own production and consumption would be sufficient to fry the planet. There is no pathway to the future that does not pass through an energy revolution in the developed world. What will this energy revolution entail?

Fossil fuels are so inextricably linked to our energy system that it will be impossible to extract them overnight. Hydroelectric power is only 6 per cent of current world energy use and nuclear power is roughly about the same. Renewable sources are only 1 per cent of the world's energy production. Energy efficiency is a large and mostly untapped resource but even it can't take us all the way to where we need to go. It is very difficult to drastically decrease the world's use of fossil fuels in the immediate term, yet this is what we need to do. This explains the interest in new technologies for capturing carbon, either emitted by fossil fuels plants or directly from the atmosphere, and storing it safely.

These technologies, however, cannot act as a substitute for taking the necessary and aggressive next steps towards weaning our energy systems off fossil fuels. To do this, we need a strong price signal – a cost of producing carbon emissions that provides the right incentives to economize on fossil fuel use. For industrialized countries the price signal comes from the cap the Kyoto Protocol imposes on their carbon emissions. For developing countries the price signal comes from Kyoto's CDM and the opportunity cost they incur for producing emissions rather than carbon offsets. The benefit of technologies for capturing and storing carbon is that they do not interfere with the price signal, as other proposed stop-gap measures will. For example, in the US there is increasing pressure to resume oil drilling in protected areas in Alaska, to ease the burden of higher energy prices until alternatives to oil can be discovered. This contradicts the rationale of climate policy and takes us further from the goal of emissions reduction. By increasing the supply of oil in the hope of lowering its price, it would undermine incentives for greater energy efficiency and investment in renewables.[17] More drilling is a stop-gap measure for higher energy prices, not a stop-gap measure for building a stable climate future.

To build a new energy infrastructure capable of delivering power from renewable and clean energy sources to our homes and our factories will take time – time we don't necessarily have. If the global community had acted sooner when the evidence of climate change emerged we might have more options now for dealing with the crisis. Waiting for new technologies to miraculously appear in the absence of a strong price signal may be like waiting for Godot. Assuming annual improvements in energy use and energy technologies leads us to a paradoxical conclusion. Because climate change is a long-term crisis and predictable, inexorable technological change will make it easier and cheaper to reduce emissions in the future, therefore it seems better to wait before addressing the problem of climate change.[18] This view of technical change leads to very cautious recommendations about how low to set our emissions caps in the near future. Waiting always seems like a better option if you believe that the problem can solve itself in time. But waiting is exactly what we cannot risk doing.

Getting the price right for carbon is the first step in combating climate change. This is why we cannot afford to let the Kyoto Protocol and its carbon market disappear after 2012 without firm caps on global emissions to strengthen and prolong the price signal. But we can only arrive in the future with new energy technologies available if we start the conscious, carefully planned development of those technologies today. Waiting for the *deus ex machina* of technical change will ensure that we face fewer options in the future at significantly higher costs.[19]

Solving the climate crisis demands concerted planned investments in research and development. We need a Manhattan Project (the joint US, UK and Canadian project to develop the first nuclear weapon during the Second World War) for developing the new energy technologies of the 21st century and a New Deal – really a Green Deal – for building the infrastructure to support it. As recent studies have shown, recycling the carbon revenues from the sale of carbon allowances in national carbon markets can actually stimulate economic growth, by redistributing income from rich to poor –

from those who save to those who spend.[20] All the while, the price signal can work its magic by offering incentives to the private sector to develop the industries of the future, and the CDM can deliver these advances to the developing world. But no country will embark on this ambitious endeavour alone, unless its efforts are nested in a larger global effort to solve climate change.

New technologies can stimulate new investment, save consumers money, stimulate productive research and development with spill-over benefits for other sectors, create new jobs and help to reduce energy imports and increase technology exports. Massive public investment in military technology since World War II led to the widespread adoption of jet aircraft, semi-conductors and the Internet by industries and households and is partly responsible for the technological advantage the US holds globally. If the rest of the world moves forwards with the Kyoto Protocol without the US, the US risks losing its technological advantage globally unless it charts (and funds) a careful and deliberate new technology path.[21]

To further complicate matters, countries such as the US must commit to solving climate change in a very precarious financial environment. Years of irresponsible deregulation of global financial markets, by the very mindset that encourages a self-regulating, cautious business-as-usual approach to climate change, has brought the global economy to its knees. This is a potentially ominous new sign for climate negotiations in Copenhagen in 2009; if the Europeans were already demonstrating signs of weakness in their commitment to Kyoto and its carbon market, they may arrive in Copenhagen on even shakier ground. Will Barack Obama be able to push through aggressive climate legislation and get the US back into the Kyoto Protocol during the worst economic crisis since the Great Depression? The last US president to acknowledge the climate crisis, Bill Clinton, was unable to do it during the roaring economy of the 1990s. The omens are not good.

The conditions are ripe for taking a leap forward. It is hard to convince people to make changes in their lives when by all outward appearances everything is fine. This has always been the difficulty: convincing people of the urgency of the climate crisis when the worst effects are still far off in the future. But now, with the global economy in a shambles, everyone recognizes the need for change. As we rebuild, it is clear that we do not want to go back to what we had before. If governments will have to spend to stimulate their economies and keep people employed in the face of a global recession, governments can also spend on transforming our energy infrastructure and building an energy system for the new millennium. As we watch major governments worldwide pour trillions of dollars into financial markets to attempt to stem the tide of losses, we are reminded that some crises are so big that government is the only actor capable of effectively responding. And as we witness the financial crisis unfold in country after country, we are reminded that the world is not quite as big as we think; we are all connected.

The magic of Kyoto is that it can avert the risk of global warming at no net cost to the global economy. Its carbon market accounts for the cost of emissions to the global environment by using an efficient free market mechanism. And Kyoto does all this without requiring any donations to support its performance. On the contrary, its carbon market creates a new source of funding for projects that promote global energy and wealth, which help close the wealth gap between rich and poor nations.

It is true that Kyoto needs updating: expanding the range of CDM clean technology projects to negative carbon technologies, reducing global emission caps as needed, including for the US, and ensuring proper treatment of developing nations' emissions through the new financial mechanisms proposed in this book. We can do that. It is possible and it will probably happen in the end.

Preserving the most unique and magical features of the Kyoto Protocol is the greatest challenge confronting us. Kyoto has the potential to unite countries, close the income divide and save us all from the risk of climate change. The question remaining is, will the global community save Kyoto?

Notes

INTRODUCTION

1   Yardley, 2007.

2   McMichael et al., 2003.

3   'Coal Power Still Powerful', *The Economist*, 15 November 2007.

4   Energy use is expected to increase five to ten times during this century (US Department of Energy). The US coal industry recently presented an energy independence plan to secure subsidies for coal production.

5   UNEP, 2008.

6   World Bank, 2008.

CHAPTER 1

1   The UN FAO's estimate of 18 per cent includes greenhouse gases released in every part of the meat production cycle. Transport, by contrast, accounts for 13 per cent of humankind's greenhouse gas footprint, according to the IPCC. *See* UN FAO, 2006 and IPCC.

2   UN IPCC, 2007.

3   Before the Industrial Revolution, atmospheric carbon dioxide levels stood at around 280 parts per million (ppm). Now it is nearly 400ppm.

4   UN IPCC, 2007.

5   Ibid.

6   Ibid.

7   OECD, 2007.

8   Pearce, 2005.

9   Smith, 2008.

10   Martin Parry, quoted in Pearce, 2005.

11   UN IPCC, 2007.

12   UN IPCC, 2007.

13   'Heat Waves Chilling Warning', *Chicago Sun Times*, 13 July 2005.

14   IPCC, 2007.

15   Kurz, 2008.

16   Bradshaw and Holzapfel, 2006.

17   OECD, 2007.

18   UN IPCC, 2007.

19   Swiss Re Economic Research and Consulting, Sigma No. 1/2008.

20   UN IPCC, 2007.

21   Ibid.

22   Martin Parry, quoted in Pearce, 2005.

23   Stern, 2006.

Notes

CHAPTER 2

1   US Department of Energy (DOE) and International Energy Agency (IEA).

2   UNEP, Global Trends in Sustainable Energy Investment 2008, 2008. Available at http://sefi.unep.org/english/globaltrends.html.

3   Carbon concentration in the atmosphere is a 'public good' as defined by economists because it is the same all over the world. The first time climate change was indentified with a public good was in Chichilnisky and Heal, 1994.

4   DeCanio, 2009.

5   Ackerman et al., 2009 and Ackerman and Heinzerling, 2004.

6   Ramsey, 1928. See also Ackerman et al, 2009 and Heal, 2000.

7   Ackerman and Heinzerling, 2004.

8   Bromley, 1992.

9   Chichilnisky and Heal, 1993.

10   Risks that are created by our own actions were introduced to the economic literature by Chichilnisky, 1996(a), an article that received the Leif Johansen's award at the University of Oslo.

11   Ackerman et al., 2009.

12   Stern, 2006. The IPCC 4th Assessment Report reviewed costs for a low stabilization target (445-535 ppm-CO_2); no study predicted more than 3 per cent of GDP. For higher stabilization targets, estimates are 2–2.5 per cent of GDP.

13   Ackerman et al., 2009.

14   Estimate of long-term costs of the Iraq war, by non-partisan Congressional Budget Office.

15   Stern, 2006.

16   Ackerman and Stanton, 2008.

17   OECD, 2007.

18   McMichael et al., 2003.

19   Estimate of Mark Sidall at Bristol University, see http://www.guardian.co.uk/science/2008/sep/01/sea.level.rise.

20   Yardley, 2007.

21   Swiss Re Economic Research and Consulting, Sigma No 1/2008.

22   Swiss Re, Sigma No 3/2008.

23   Ibid.

24   Swiss Re Economic Research and Consulting, Sigma No 1/2008.

25   Stern, 2006 and IPCC, 2007.

26   Chichilnisky, 2009(a), World Bank, 2006, 2007.

27   Chichilnisky and Eisenberger, 2007 and 2009.

28   Wind, biomass, hydroelectric, solar, geothermal, nuclear and possibly fusion.

29   By the end of this century, it is expected to be five to ten times today's energy use. US DOE.

30   89 per cent of the energy used today comes from fossil fuels; less than 1 per cent from renewable sources; 0.01 per cent is solar energy.

31   Cohen et al., 2009 and Eisenberger and Chichilnisky, 2007, 2009.

32   Scientists consider the possibility of a 'tipping point', a level of heating that triggers catastrophic climate change, which is typical of physical systems with complex feedback effects. The earth's climate is generally believed to be one of them. In general, one views the risks as having 'heavy tails' so rare events turn out to be more frequent than usually expected.

33   Transitioning away from fossil fuels in a short period of time could lead to social disruption, since most human life is dependent on energy.

34   Chichilnisky and Eisenberger, 2007 and 2009, US DOE.

35   Jones, 2008, 2009, Eisenberger and Chichilnisky, 2007, 2009. Simultaneous production of electricity and air capture is called 'cogeneration'.

36   Cohen et al., 2009, Chichilnisky, 2008(a).

37   Eisenberger and Chichilnisky, 2007, 2009.

CHAPTER 3

1   Tyndall, 1861.

2   Chichilnisky, 1977(a) and 1977(b).

3   Article 2, p9, UNFCC, 1992.

4   UNFCCC, 1992.

5   Chichilnisky and Heal, 1995, Chichilnisky, 1994(b).

6   Chichilnisky, 1997.

7   See Chichilnisky Pegram Lectures on www.chichilnisky.com 'Books and writings'.

8   Cap-and-trade systems cap global emissions and bind the emissions rights of polluters. Awarding emissions rights on the basis of past emissions levels is often called 'grandfathering'.

9   Hourcade, 2002. The CDM allows credits for industrial nations' projects that are carried out on developing nations' soil and are proven to reduce emissions. These can be traded in the carbon market. This was my preferred approach to how to integrate developing nations into the Kyoto Protocol carbon market while still abiding by the Article 4 of the UNFCC, which does not allow limits on developing nations' emissions without compensation. I ran a conference on this topic at Columbia University with the negotiators of the Kyoto Protocol in 1997–1998: 'From Kyoto to Buenos Aires: Technology Transfer and Carbon Trading'. Ambassadors Kilaparti Ramakrishna and Raul Estrada Oyuela participated as main speakers, among others.

CHAPTER 4

1   Bart Chilton, quoted by Reuters News 25 June 2008.

2   Chichilnisky, 2009(b), Sheeran 2006(a), Chichilnisky and Heal, 1994, 2000.

3   Adam Smith described how market forces – the invisible hand – can harness individual self-interest for the greater social good. See Smith, 1776.

4   UNEP, 2008.

5   Estrada Oyuela, 2000. The climatic last minute addition was the carbon market and its attendant CDM.

6   Article 2, UNFCCC, 1992.

Notes

7 Countries were to reduce their emissions to 1990 levels by 2000. Since 1990, emissions in the US have actually increased by more than 15 per cent.

8 Estrada Oyuela, 2000.

9 Article 3, The Kyoto Protocol to the UNFCCC, 1997.

10 The Kyoto Protocol CDM provides incentives to curb deforestation in developing countries under certain conditions.

11 Article 2.3. See Estrada Oyuela, 2000.

12 Chichilnisky and Heal, 1994, 2000, Sheeran, 2006. This is not true for sulphur dioxide.

13 This was the rationale proposed by Chichilnisky in her introduction of a carbon market with a preferential treatment for developing nations. See Chichilnisky, 1997, Chichilnisky and Heal, 1994 and 1995.

14 Chichilnisky and Heal, 1995.

15 Ibid.

16 The figure on p5 provides a breakdown for industrial and developing nations.

17 This includes all kinds of meat. The OECD's consumption of the world's beef and veal alone is about 80 per cent. See also Chichilnisky, 2005–2006 and UN FAO, 2006.

18 UN Food and Agriculture Association, 2006.

19 Chichilnisky and Heal, 1994, 1995 and 2000, Chichilnisky 2009(b) and 1994.

20 Chichilnisky and Heal, 1994, 1995 and 2000.

21 Chichilnisky, 2009(c)

22 Estrada Oyuela, 2000.

23 See 'Status and Trends of the Carbon Market', World Bank Report, 2006 and 2007.

24 Estrada Oyuela, 2000. The Kyoto Protocol does not limit the amount of purchased carbon reduction credits a country can use to meet its emissions cap. It does, however, state that: 'trading shall be supplemental to domestic actions for the purpose of meeting quantified emission limitation and reduction commitments'. There are further restrictions on the use of specific types of CDM project as well.

25 Chichilnisky and Heal, 1994, 1995 and 2000.

26 World Bank, 2006, 2007.

27 Ibid.

28 Ibid.

29 Ibid.

CHAPTER 5

1 The United Nations Regional Information Centre for Western Europe Magazine, Issue No. 16, December 2007.

2 Chichilnisky presented this proposal at the following: the Bali COP on 13 December 2007; the International Monetary Fund in July and October 2007; a Bipartisan Briefing in Capitol Hill organized at US Congress by Rep. Michael Honda in May 2008, with the participation and support of seven Members of the House; at the Parliament in Victoria, Australia, in November 2008; at a Caucus on Sustainable Energy and the Environment

in Capitol Hill, with the participation of 42 Members of the US House of Representatives, on 31 March 2009; and at the UNCTAD Expert Meeting on Trade and Investment Opportunities and Challenges under the Clean Development Mechanism in Geneva, 27–29 April 2009.

3   Campbell, 2008.

4   Related to 'clean coal' proposals to produce electricity from coal in a carbon neutral way through CCS technologies (*see* www.nma.org/ccs/aboutccs.asp). *See* US DOE information on ongoing projects.

5   Chichilnisky and Eisenberger, 2007, 2009, Jones, 2008, 2009, Chichilnisky, 2008(a), and Cohen, Change, Chichilnisky, Eisenberger P. and Eisenberger N., 2008.

6   Tollefson, 2008.

7   World Bank, 2006–2007.

8   Tollefson, 2008.

9   'Tough Talks on EU's Climate Plan' BBC News, 20 October 2008.

10   Quote from Arthur Runge-Metzger who oversees climate issues at the EC: 'The EC needs to spur new technologies now, because paying for offsets elsewhere won't solve the problem', quoted in Tollefson, 2008. Paying for offsets elsewhere (in developing nations) is the nature of the CDM.

11   Miles Austin, head of the European regulatory affairs for carbon offset dealer Ecosecurities, Dublin.

12   OECD, 2007.

13   'Coal Power Still Powerful', *The Economist*, 15 November 2007.

14   Buckley, 2008.

15   On 12 November 2008, Chichilnisky addressed Members of Parliament in Melbourne, Australia on the commercial benefits of the carbon market.

16   World Bank, 2008.

17   IPCC, 2007.

18   Chichilnisky, 2009(a).

19   Energy Information Agency (EIA) http://www.eia.doe.gov/environment.html

20   Milanovic, 2006.

21   World Bank, 2008.

22   Baumert and Kete, 2002.

23   Zhang, 1999.

24   Biagini, 2000.

25   Buckley, 2008.

26   Chichilnisky, 1994(a).

27   Chichilnisky, 1981.

28   Chichilnisky, 1981 and Rodrick, 2006.

29   Chichilnisky, 1995.

30   Chichilnisky, 1994(a).

Notes

CHAPTER 6

1   Ackerman and Stanton, 2006 and Stern, 2006.

2   World Bank, 2006, 2007.

3   For the critical timing issue see the 2006 Stern Review.

4   Boyce and Riddle, 2007, as well as Office of Congressional Research and other scholarly works.

5   World Bank, 2006, 2007.

6   UNFCCC CDM http://cdm.UNFCCCc.int/about/index.html

7   Project descriptions at UNFCCC at http://cdm.UNFCCCc.int/Projects/projsearch.html.

8   Chichilnisky and Heal, 1994, 1995, 2000, Sheeran, 2006(a).

9   Sheeran, 2006(b).

CHAPTER 7

1   Potter, 2008.

2   Chichilnisky and Wu, 2006 predicted exactly this phenomenon a year before it started. See also Chichilnisky, 2008.

3   Chichilnisky and Wu, 2006 provides a rigorous demonstration of this proposition.

4   Chichilnisky, 2008(b).

5   International Energy Agency, 2008.

6   Chichilnisky is working in a commercial demonstration plant for one of the negative carbon technologies available today, with physicists and business people in the US.

7   UN Millennium Report, 2000.

8   Chichilnisky, 1998.

9   Ibid.

10   Ibid.

11   Ibid.

12   Ibid.

13   The Global Forest Resources Assessment, UN FAO, 2005

14   Sukhdev, 2008.

15   Black, 2008.

16   Chichilnisky, 2009(a).

17   Increased drilling in Alaska will not have a perceptible impact on global oil prices since the resulting increase in supply from drilling will be small relative to current world supplies.

18   Ackerman et al., 2009.

19   Ibid.

20   Boyce and Riddle, 2007.

21   Ackerman et al., 2009.

Bibliography

Ackerman, Frank, DeCanio, Stephen J., Howarth, Richard and Sheeran, Kristen A., 'The Limitations of Integrated Assessment Models of Climate Change', *Climatic Change*. Forthcoming 2009.

Ackerman, Frank and Stanton, Elisabeth, 'The Costs of Climate Change: What We'll Pay if Climate Change Continues Unchecked', 2008. Available at http://www.nrdc.org/globalwarming/cost/fcost.pdf.

Ackerman, Frank and Stanton, Elisabeth, 'Climate Change – The Costs of Inaction', 2006. Available at http://www.foe.co.uk/resource/reports/econ_costs_cc.pdf

Ackerman, Frank and Heinzerling, Lisa, *Priceless*, The New Press, 2004.

Baumert, Kevin A. and Kete, Nancy, 'Will Developing Countries Carbon Emissions Swamp Global Emissions Reduction Efforts?', World Resources Institute 2002.

Biagini, B., (ed), *Confronting Climate Change: Economic Priorities and Climate Protection in Developing Nations*. Washington, DC: National Environmental Trust, 2000.

Black, Richard, 'Nature loss "dwarfs bank crisis"', BBC News, 10 October 2008.

Boyce, James and Riddle, Matthew, 'Cap and Rebate: How to Curb Global Warming while Protecting the Incomes of American Families', Political Economy Research Institute Working Paper No. 150, 2007.

Bradshaw, William E. and Holzapfel, C., Perspectives Section, Science, June 2006.

Bromley, Daniel W., *Making the Commons Work*. San Francisco, ICS Press, 1992.

Buckley, Chris, 'China Report Warns of Greenhouse Gas Leap' Reuters News Service, 22 October 2008.

Campbell, Warren, *Reducing Carbon Capture and Storage: Assessing the Economics*, McKinsey & Company, 2008. Available at http://www.mckinsey.com/clientservice/ccsi/pdf/CCS_Assessing_the_Economics.pdf

Chichilnisky, Graciela, a) *Beyond the Global Divide: From Basic Needs to the Knowledge Revolution*. Forthcoming, 2009.

Chichilnisky, Graciela, (ed), b) *The Economics of Climate Change*, Edward Elgar, Library of Critical Writings in Economics, 2009.

Chichilnisky, Graciela c), 'Le Paradoxe des Marches Verts' Les Echos, 21 January 2009, http://www.lesechos.fr/info/analyses/4822817-le-paradoxe-des-marches-verts.htm

Chichilnisky, Graciela, a) 'Energy Security, Economic Development and Climate Change: Short and Long Term Challenges,' El Boletin Informativo Techint No. 325, April 2008, p53–76.

Chichilnisky, Graciela, b) 'How to Restore the Stability and Health of the Economy', 2008. Available at http://www.huffingtonpost.com/graciela-chichilnisky/its-the-mortgages-how-to_b_144376.html

Chichilnisky, Graciela, 'Economics Returns from the Biosphere', Nature, Vol. 391, 12 February 1998, p629–630.

Chichilnisky, Graciela, 'Development and Global Finance: The Case for an International Bank for Environmental Settlements', Report No. 10, United Nations Development Program and the United Nations Educational Scientific and Cultural Organization, May 1997.

Chichilnisky, Graciela, a) 'Markets with Endogenous Uncertainty: Theory and Policy' Theory and Decision, Vol. 41, 1996, p91–131.

Chichilnisky, Graciela, b) 'The Greening of Bretton Woods', Financial Times 10 January, 1996.

Chichilnisky, Graciela, 'The Economic Value of the Earth's Resources' Invited

Bibliography

Perspectives Article, Trends in Ecology and Evolution (TREE), 1995–96, p135–140.

Chichilnisky, Graciela, a) 'North–South Trade and the Global Environment', *American Economic Review*, Vol. 84, No. 4, 1994, p851–874.

Chichilnisky, Graciela b) 'The Trading of Carbon Emissions in Industrial and Developing Nations' in Jones (ed.) *The Economics of Climate Change*, OECD Paris, 1994.

Chichilnisky, Graciela, 'Terms of Trade and Domestic Distribution: Export Led Growth with Abundant Labor' *Journal of Development Economics*, Vol 8, 1981, p163–192.

Chichilnisky, Graciela, a) 'Economic Development and Efficiency Criteria in the Satisfaction of Basic Needs' *Applied Mathematical Modeling*, Vol. 1, No.6, September 1977, p290–297.

Chichilnisky, Graciela, b) 'Development Patterns and the International' *Journal of International Affairs*, Vol. 1, No. 2, 1977, p274–304.

Chichilnisky, Graciela and Eisenberger, Peter, 'Energy Security, Economic Development and Global Warming: Addressing Short and Long Term Challenges' *The Economics of Climate Change*, Graciela Chichilnisky (ed.), Edward Elgar, 2009.

Chichilnisky, Graciela and Heal, Geoffrey, *Environmental Markets: Equity and Efficiency*, Columbia University Press, 2000.

Chichilnisky, Graciela and Heal, Geoffrey, Markets for Tradeable CO_2 Emissions Quotas: *Principles and Practice*, OECD Report No. 153, OECD Paris, 1995.

Chichilnisky, Graciela and Heal, Geoffrey, 'Who Should Abate Carbon Emissions: An International Perspective' *Economic Letters*, Spring 1994, p443–449.

Chichilnisky, Graciela and Heal, Geoffrey, 'Global Environmental Risks' *Journal of Economic Perspectives*, Vol. 7 (4), 1993, p65–86.

Chichilnisky, Graciela and Wu, H.M., 'General Equilibrium with Endogenous Uncertainty and Default', *Journal of Mathematical Economics*, Vol. 42, 2006.

Cohen, R, Chance, G, Chichilnisky, Graciela, Eisenberger, Peter, and Eisenberger, Nicholas, 'Global Warming and Carbon-Negative Technology' Working Paper, Princeton 2008, to appear in *Journal of Energy & Environment*.

DeCanio, Stephen J., 'The Political Economy of Global Carbon Emissions Reduction' *Ecological Economics*, No. 68, 2009, p915–924.

Eisenberger, Peter and Chichilnisky, Graciela, *Reducing the Risk of Climate Change While Producing Renewable Energy*, Columbia University, May 2007

Estrada Oyuela, Raul, 2000. 'A Commentary on the Kyoto Protocol' in *Environmental Markets: Equity and Efficiency*, Graciela Chichilnisky and Geoffrey Heal (eds), 2000.

Heal, Geoffrey, *Valuing the Future*, Columbia University Press, 2000.

Hourcade, J.C. and Ghersi, F., 'The Economics of a Lost Deal: Kyoto – The Hague – Marrakesh', *The Energy Journal*, Vol. 23, No. 3, 2002.

International Energy Agency (IEA), *Carbon Dioxide Capture and Storage: A Key Carbon Abatement Option*, 2008.

Jones, Nicola, 'Sucking Carbon Out of Air' *Nature News*, 17 December 2008.

Jones, Nicola, 'Sucking It Up' *Nature*, Vol. 458, April 2009.

Kurz, W.A., et al., 'Mountain pine beetle and forest carbon feedback to climate change', *Nature* Vol. 452, 2008, p987–990.

McMichael, A.J. et al., *Climate Change and Human Health*. World Health Organization, 2003.

Milanovic, Branko, 'Global Income Inequality: A Review' *World Economics* Vol. 7 No. 1, 2006.

OECD *Ranking of the World's Cities Most Exposed to Coastal Flooding Today and in the Future*, extract from OECD Environment Working Paper No. 1, OECD, Paris, 2007. Available at:

http://www.oecd.org/dataoecd/16/10/39721444.pdf

Pearce, Fred, 'Climate Warning as Siberia Melts' New Scientist, 11 August 2005.

Potter, Mitch, 'The Dawn of the Green Age is Delayed', The Toronto Star, 28 October 2008.

Ramsey, Frank P., 'A Mathematical Theory of Saving' Economic Journal, 1928, Vol. 38, No. 152, p543–559.

Rodrick, Dan, 'Sea Change in the World Economy' article prepared for Techint Conference August 30 2005, Techint Report 2006.

Sheeran, Kristen A., a) 'Who Should Abate Carbon Emissions: A Note' Environmental & Resource Economics, Vol. 35, 2006, p89–98.

Sheeran, Kristen A., b) 'Side Payments Or Exemptions: The Implications for Equitable and Efficient Climate Control' Eastern Economic Journal, Vol. 32, Issue 2, 2006.

Smith, Adam, An Inquiry Into the Nature and Causes of the Wealth of Nations, 1776.

Smith, Lewis, 'Wildlife gives early warning of "deadly dozen" diseases spread by climate change', Times, 8 October 2008 (UK).

Stern, Nicholas, The Economics of Climate Change: The Stern Review. 2006 Available at: http://www.hmtreasury.gov.uk/independent_ reviews/stern_review_economics_climate_ change/stern_review_report.cfm.

Sukhdev, Pavan, The Economics of Ecosystems and Biodiversity, 2008. Available at: http://ec.europa.eu/environment/nature/bio diversity/economics/index_en.htm

Swiss Re Economic Research and Consulting, Natural Catastrophes and Man-made Disasters in 2007, Sigma No. 1, 2008.

Swiss Re Economic Research and Consulting, World Insurance 2007: Emerging Markets Leading the Way, Sigma No. 3, 2008.

Tollefson, Jeff, 'Carbon Trading Market has Uncertain Future', Nature, April 2008, p508.

Tyndall, John 'On the Absorption and Radiation of Heat by Gases and Vapors and on the Physical Connexion of Radiation Absorption and Conduction' Transactions of the Royal Society of London, Vol 151, Part 2, 1861, pp1–36. The Bakevian Lecture London: Taylor and Francis 1861.

United Nations Environment Program (UNEP), Global Trends in Sustainable Energy Investment 2008, 2008. Available at: http://sefi.unep.org/english/globaltrends.html

United Nations Food and Agriculture Organization (FAO), Livestock's Long Shadow, 2006. Available at: http://www.fao.org/ docrep/010/a0701e/a0701e00.htm

United Nations, United Nations Framework Convention on Climate Change, 1992. Available at: http://www2.onep.go.th/CDM/en/UNFCCCTe xt_Eng.pdf

United Nations Intergovernmental Panel on Climate Change (IPCC), Climate Change 2007: Synthesis Report. Contribution of Working Groups I, II and III to the Fourth Assessment Report of the Intergovernmental Panel on Climate Change, Pachauri, R.K and Reisinger, A. (eds), 2007.

United Nations, The Kyoto Protocol to the United Nations Framework Convention on Climate Change, 1997. Available at: http:// unfccc.int/resource/docs/convkp/kpeng.pdf

World Bank, State and Trends of the Carbon Market, 2006

World Bank, State and Trends of the Carbon Market, 2007

World Bank, World Development Indicators 2008.

Yardley, William 'Engulfed by Climate Change, Town Seeks Lifeline', New York Times, 27 May 2007.

Zhang, Z., 'Is China Taking Actions to Limit Greenhouse Gas Emissions? Past Evidence and Future Prospects', Promoting Development While Limiting Greenhouse Gas Emissions: Trends and Baselines, Reid, W.V. and Goldemberg, J., (eds.) New York: UNDP and WRI, 1999.

Glossary of Terms

Adaptive capacity: The capability of a country or region, including on an institutional level, to implement effective adaptation measures.

Allocation: The giving of emissions permits or allowances to greenhouse gas emitters to establish an emissions trading market. The division of permits/allowances can also be done through the grandfathering method and/or auctioning.

Annex I: The term used for the 24 industrialized countries that in 1992 were members of the Organization for Economic Cooperation and Development (OECD) and the 14 countries that at the time were in the middle of a transition from a centrally-controlled planned economy to a market economy, including the former Eastern Bloc countries. The European Union (EU) is also in this group. Several countries have subsequently joined, so the group now numbers 41 countries (including the EU).

Annex II: Annex II countries are the same as in Annex I apart from the transition economies. Annex II countries undertake to pay a share of the costs of the developing countries' reductions in emissions.

Annex B: Annex B in the Kyoto Protocol lists those developed countries that have agreed to a commitment to control their greenhouse gas emissions in the period 2008–12,including those in the OECD, Central and Eastern Europe and the Russian Federation. The latest list of Annex B countries (2007) matches that of Annex I, with the exclusion of Turkey.

The Association of Southeast Asian Nations (ASEAN): Established on 8 August 1967 in Bangkok by the five original Member Countries: Indonesia, Malaysia, Philippines, Singapore and Thailand. Brunei Darussalam joined in 1984, Vietnam in 1995, Lao PDR and Myanmar in 1997 and Cambodia in 1999. The ASEAN Declaration states that the aims and purposes of the Association are: (1) to accelerate economic growth, social progress and cultural development in the region and (2) to promote regional peace and stability through abiding respect for justice and the rule of law in the relationship among countries in the region and adherence to the principles of the United Nations Charter.

Biofuel: Gas or liquid fuel made from plant material. The source materials can include wood, wood waste, wood liquors, peat, wood sludge, agricultural waste, straw, tires, fish oils, tall oil, sludge waste, waste alcohol, municipal solid waste and landfill gases. The most common form of biofuel at present is ethanol blended into petrol.

Cap and trade: A cap and trade system is an emissions trading system where total emissions are limited or 'capped'. The Kyoto Protocol is a cap and trade system in the sense that emissions from Annex B countries are capped and that excess permits might be traded.

Carbon: A basic chemical element in all organic compounds. When combusted, it is transformed into carbon dioxide – one tonne of carbon generates about 2.5 tonnes of carbon dioxide.

Carbon (dioxide) capture and storage (CCS): A process consisting of the separation of carbon dioxide from industrial and energy-related sources, transport to a storage location and long-term isolation from the atmosphere (for example, long term storage in oil wells or aquifers).

Carbon dioxide (CO_2): A naturally occurring,

colourless, odourless gas that is a normal part of the atmosphere. It is created through respiration, as well in the decay or combustion of animal and vegetable matter. It is also a by-product of burning fossil fuels from fossilized carbon deposits, such as oil, gas and coal, as well as some industrial processes. Because it traps heat radiated by the Earth into the atmosphere, it is called a greenhouse gas, and is a major factor in potential climate change. It is one of the six greenhouse gases that current climate science recommends be cut. Other greenhouse gases are measured in relation to the global warming potential (GWP) of carbon dioxide, and are measured in carbon dioxide equivalent (CO_2e).

Carbon neutral: The concept of calculating your emissions, reducing them where possible, and then offsetting the remainder. It also refers to a voluntary market mechanism for addressing CO_2 emissions from sources not yet addressed by climate policy (such as private households, air travel etc.).

Carbon sequestration: The process whereby carbon dioxide is absorbed in such a manner as to prevent its release into the atmosphere. It can be stored underground (see CCS) or stored in a carbon sink, such as a forest, the soil or in the ocean.

Carbon tax: A tax by governments, usually on the use of carbon-containing fuels, but can be implemented as a levy on all product-associated carbon emissions.

Certified Emission Reduction (CER): A credit or unit equal to one tonne of carbon dioxide equivalent, generated under the CDM. The unit is defined in article 12 of the Kyoto Protocol and may be used by countries listed in Annex I of the Kyoto Protocol towards meeting their binding emission reduction and limitation commitments.

Chicago Climate Exchange (CCX): The Chicago Climate Exchange is North America's only voluntary, legally binding greenhouse gas (GHG) reduction and trading system for emission sources and offset projects. CCX employs independent verification, includes six greenhouse gases, and has been trading greenhouse gas emission allowances since 2003. The companies joining the exchange commit to reducing their aggregate emissions by 6% by 2010.

Clean Development Mechanism (CDM): This is the mechanism laid out in article 12 of the Kyoto Protocol, that allows Annex I parties to the Kyoto Protocol to make emissions reductions in Annex II countries.

Climate change: This is a term referring to a change in the state of the climate, used to imply a significant change from one climatic condition to another. Note that the UNFCCC, in its article 1, defines climate change as: 'a change of climate which is attributed directly or indirectly to human activity that alters the composition of the global atmosphere and which is in addition to natural climate variability observed over comparable time periods'. The UNFCCC thus makes a distinction between climate change attributable to human activities altering the atmospheric composition, and climate variability attributable to natural causes.

Conference of the Parties (COP): The COP is the supreme body of the UNFCCC.

Commodity: Something of value that can be bought or sold, usually a product or raw material (lumber, wheat, coffee, metals).

Energy efficiency: The ratio of the useful output of services from an article of industrial equipment to the energy use by such an article; for example, the number of operational hours of a filling machine per kW

Glossary of Terms

hour used, or vehicle miles travelled per gallon of fuel (mpg).

European Union (EU): The European Union is an economic and political union of 27 member states, located primarily in Europe. It was established by the Treaty of Maastricht on 1 November 1993 upon the foundations of the pre-existing European Economic Community. The EU has developed a single market through a standardized system of laws that apply in all member states, guaranteeing the freedom of movement of people, goods, services and capital. It maintains a common trade policy, agricultural and fisheries policies and a regional development policy.

European Union Emissions Trading Scheme (EU ETS): The European Union Emissions Trading System is the largest multinational emissions trading scheme in the world. It currently covers more than 10,000 installations in the energy and industrial sectors, which are collectively responsible for close to half of the EU's emissions of CO_2 and 40% of its total greenhouse gas emissions.

Framework Convention: Convention that provides a decision-making and organizational framework for the adoption of subsequent complementary agreements (such as a Protocol). Usually contains substantial provisions of a general nature, the details of which can be provided in the subsequent agreements.

Grandfathering: Grandfathering refers to a particular pattern of distibuting the rights to pollute. When pollution rights are grandfathered, existing polluters are typically allocated their permits in some proportion to their past emissions levels or emissions activity.

Gross Domestic Product (GDP): The monetary value of all goods and services produced within a nation.

Group of Seven (G7): Now the Group of Eight (G8). See definition below.

Group of Eight (G8): Formerly the Group of Seven (G7). An informal group of some of the world's largest economies, it was originally set up following the oil shocks and global economic recession of the 1970s. The Group consists of France, Germany, Italy, the UK, Japan, Canada, the US and Russia. The leaders of each country meet every year to discuss how best to manage global economic challenges. The European Union is represented at the G8 by the president of the European Commission and by the leader of the country that holds the EU presidency but it does not officially take part in G8 political discussions.

Group of 77 and China (G77/China): The developing country group in the climate negotiations, consisting of more than 130 developing countries.

Host Country: A host country is the country where a JI or CDM project is physically located. A project has to be approved by host country to receive CERs.

Intergovernmental Panel on Climate Change (IPCC): The IPCC was established by the World Meteorological Organisation (WMO) and the United Nations Environmental Programme (UNEP) in 1988 to review scientific, technical and socio-economic information relevant for the understanding of climate change, its potential impacts and options for adaptation and mitigation. It is open to all Members of the UN and of WMO. This panel involves over 2,000 of the world's climate experts and the majority of the climate change facts and future predictions covered come from information reviewed by the IPCC.

Joint Initiative: Mechanism of the Kyoto Protocol that allows Annex I parties to the protocol to generate emissions reductions through the development of projects in other developed countries (such as Eastern Europe).

Joint Implementation (JI): A mechanism for transfer of emissions permits from one Annex B country to another.

Keidanren Voluntary Action Plan: An environment action plan devised by the Japan Business Federation aimed at stabilizing CO2 emissions from fuel combustion and industrial processes at 1990 levels by 2010. This plan is included in the Kyoto Protocol Target Achievement Plan of Japan, but there is no agreement with the government to assure the targets are reached. The plan makes no commitment to the Japanese government that the target will be met.

Kyoto Protocol: The Kyoto Protocol to the UNFCCC was adopted in 1997 in Kyoto, Japan, at the Third Session of the Conference of the Parties (COP) to the UNFCCC. It contains legally binding commitments, in addition to those included in the UNFCCC. Countries included in Annex B of the Protocol agreed to reduce their anthropogenic greenhouse gas emissions (carbon dioxide, methane, nitrous oxide, hydrofluorocarbons, perfluorocarbons and sulphur hexafluoride) by at least 5% below 1990 levels in the commitment period 2008 to 2012. The Kyoto Protocol entered into force on 16 February 2005.

Montreal Protocol: The Montreal Protocol on Substances that Deplete the Ozone Layer was adopted in Montreal in 1987 and subsequently adjusted and amended in London (1990), Copenhagen (1992), Vienna (1995), Montreal (1997) and Beijing (1999). It controls the consumption and production of chlorine- and bromine-containing chemicals that destroy stratospheric ozone, such as CFCs, methyl chloroform, carbon tetrachloride, and many others.

New South Wales Greenhouse Gas Abatement Market (NSW): The New South Wales market was the first regulated emissions trading market. New South Wales is Australia's oldest and most populous state. The NSW Greenhouse Gas Abatement Scheme is a state-level program designed to reduce emissions from the energy sector through carbon trading. Under the scheme, NSW energy producers are bound to emit no greater then their share of the NSW per capita emissions target. The target was set at 8.65 tonnes of CO2 equivalent in 2003, decreasing by about 3% each year thereafter through to 2007, when it will remain at 7.27. Energy producers exceeding their allotment of emissions can offset them either by surrendering NSW Greenhouse Abatement Certificates (NGACs) purchased from others in the scheme, or by paying an $11/tonne fine.

Non-Annex 1 countries: Typically developing countries that have ratified the convention.

North America Free Trade Agreement (NAFTA): The North American Free Trade Agreement was signed in 1992 between the United States, Mexico and Canada. It is an agreement to remove almost all tariff and non-tariff barriers to trade between the three countries.

Organization for Economic Cooperation and Development (OECD): an internataional organization of 30 developed countries worldwide. The OECD provides a setting where governments compare policy experiences, seek answers to common problems, identify good practice and coordinate domestic and international policies.

Regional Greenhouse Gas Initiative (RGGI): The first mandatory, market-based effort in the United States to reduce greenhouse gas emissions. Ten Northeastern and Mid-Atlantic

Glossary of Terms

states will cap and then reduce CO_2 emissions from the power sector by 10% by 2018. States will sell emission allowances through auctions and invest proceeds in consumer benefits: energy efficiency, renewable energy and other clean energy technologies.

Reinsurance: Insurance for insurance companies. It is a way of transferring or 'ceding' some of the financial risk insurance companies assume in insuring cars, homes and businesses to another insurance company, the reinsurer.

Reservoir: A component of the climate system, other than the atmosphere, which has the capacity to store, accumulate or release a substance of concern, e.g. carbon, a greenhouse gas or a precursor. Oceans, soils and forests are examples of reservoirs of carbon. Pool is an equivalent term (note that the definition of pool often includes the atmosphere). The absolute quantity of substance of concerns, held within a reservoir at a specified time, is called the stock.

Resources: This term refers to the raw materials, supplies, capital equipment, factories, offices, labour, management and entrepreneurial skills that are used in producing goods and services. It also refers to the substances that support life and fulfil human needs, including air, land, water, minerals, fossil fuels, forests and sunlight.

Sinks: A sink refers to a pool or reservoir that can absorb and hold onto significant amounts of carbon dioxide. It can refer to the removal of greenhouse gases (GHGs) from the atmosphere through land management and forestry activities that may be subtracted from a country's allowable level of emissions.

Sustainable development: This deals with meeting the needs of the present without compromising the ability of future generations to meet their needs. It is most commonly used in economic terms, to refer to economic development that takes full account of the environmental consequences of economic activity and is based on the use of resources that can be replaced or renewed and therefore are not depleted. For example, environmentally friendly forms of economic growth activities (agriculture, logging, manufacturing, etc.) that allow the continued production of a commodity without damage to the ecosystem (soil, water supplies, biodiversity or other surrounding resources).

Tipping point: The level of magnitude of a system process at which sudden or rapid change occurs. A point or level at which new properties emerge in an ecological, economic or other system, invalidating predictions based on mathematical relationships that apply at lower levels.

United Nations Framework Convention on Climate Change (UNFCC): The Convention was adopted on 9 May 1992 in New York and signed at the 1992 Earth Summit in Rio de Janeiro by more than 150 countries and the European Community. Its ultimate objective is the 'stabilization of greenhouse gas concentrations in the atmosphere at a level that would prevent dangerous anthropogenic interference with the climate system'. It contains commitments for all Parties. Under the Convention, Parties included in Annex I aim to return greenhouse gas emissions not controlled by the Montreal Protocol to 1990 levels by the year 2000. The convention entered into force in March 1994.

Index

Major page references are in **bold**

Index

Index

Index